THE REVOLUTION
AGAINST WAR

THE REVOLUTION AGAINST WAR:

SELECTED WRITINGS ON WAR AND PEACE

ROBERT S. HARTMAN

EDITED BY CLIFFORD G. HURST, PHD

IZZARD INK PUBLISHING COMPANY
P.O. Box 522251
Salt Lake City, Utah 84152
www.izzardink.com

Library of Congress Cataloging-in-Publication Data

Names: Hartman, Robert S., 1910-1973, author. | Hurst, Clifford G.
   (Clifford Guin), 1953- editor.
Title: The revolution against war : selected writings on war and peace /
   Robert S. Hartman ; edited by Clifford G. Hurst.
Description: First edition. | Salt Lake City, Utah : Izzard Ink Publishing,
   2020.
Identifiers: LCCN 2020028310 | ISBN 9781642280395 (trade paperback) | ISBN
   9781642280401 (hardback) | ISBN 9781642280388 (ebook)
Subjects: LCSH: War (Philosophy) | Peace (Philosophy) | War. | Peace.
Classification: LCC B105.W3 H38 2020 | DDC 327.1/72--dc23
LC record available at https://lccn.loc.gov/2020028310

Cover Design by Treadaway Co.
Cover Photograph in the Public Domain (U.S. Navy photo QUA.2013-11.06.02 from the
U.S. Navy Naval History and Heritage Command)
Book Design by LaceyAnn Kisko Design

First Edition August, 2020

Contact the author at info@izzardink.com

"It is nonsensical to speak of nuclear war. There is only nuclear world destruction."

— ROBERT S. HARTMAN

CONTENTS

FOREWORD

by Clifford G. Hurst, PhD

Robert S. Hartman [1910-1973] is best known today—to the extent that he is known—for his development of the Hartman Value Profile (HVP). While the HVP is increasingly being used by consultants, counselors, and executive coaches around the globe, the theory on which it is based—Hartman's theory of formal axiology—remains unfamiliar to many people. It deserves a broader audience.

Hartman's intellectual pursuits extended far beyond this theory and this instrument. He also wrote about, and advocated for, employee benefits, profit sharing, new forms of capitalism, new approaches to international relations, nuclear disarmament, spirituality, and world peace.

Hartman was a prolific writer, but many of his best thoughts never saw the light of day during his lifetime.

Shortly after Hartman's unexpected and untimely death in 1973, his widow, Rita Hartman, wrote to their friend John Davis:

> "I can comprehend that the life I helped to build has reached an end, but what overwhelms me and hurts more than anything else is to see the abundance of unfinished publications lying fallow. I am almost obsessed with the idea that somehow this must be utilized, it must go on, it must be used."

In 1976 the Robert S. Hartman Institute for Formal and Applied Axiology was founded as a not-for-profit corporation in order to preserve, refine, advance, and make better known to the world the work begun by Hartman. See the Institute's website: www.hartmaninstitute.org, for a complete statement of its mission and purpose.

Hartman's autobiography, Freedom to Live, was published posthumously by the Institute in 1994. A second edition was published in 2013. Its re-publication marked the first volume in the planned Hartman Institute Axiological Studies series. In April of 2019 the Institute published Hartman's Five Lectures in Formal Axiology.

The current and future monographs in this series continue the Institute's intention to fulfill Rita Hartman's wishes that this work "must go on."

CLIFFORD G. HURST
Editor

PREFACE

Robert Hartman's life was marked by war. As he remarks in the chapter in this collection on "The Triumph of Gravitation," his earliest recollections of childhood are those of war.

As most of the readers of this volume already know, at the age of 23, Hartman escaped from Germany shortly after Hitler was elected to power in 1933. He escaped first to England and then to Sweden. He emigrated once again as the Nazi war engine threatened Sweden. This time he emigrated, first to Mexico, then to the United States, arriving in the U.S. in 1941 at the eve of this country's involvement in what had by then become known as World War II. At that war's end, the moral consequences of the development and use of the atomic bomb disturbed him deeply. It dramatically altered his ever-evolving thoughts on war and peace, as evidenced by several essays in this collection. So, too, did the Cold War, especially the Cuban Missile Crisis, affect his thinking.

I conceptually cluster Hartman's thoughts regarding war and peace as having developed in three stages:

1. The first stage dealt with the cultural and political processes by which Hitler rose to power and by which he upended world peace. These events shook Hartman deeply and his ruminations about those events offer many lessons to readers today.

2. A second stage relates to his analysis of the horrible deaths and suffering imposed on people by World War II. His writings during the

war reveal his determination that the political regimes of Germany and Japan ought to be completely defeated through military force. Only then could restoration and rehabilitation of their societies begin.

3. Then, Hiroshima and Nagasaki happened. The detonation of the world's first atomic bombs created a new and fearful reality for humankind. War, Hartman concluded, can no longer be a rational response to human conflict. The reader can follow the gradual development of his radical, but entirely rational conclusion that the age of national sovereignty needs to come to an end. To speak of nuclear defense, he says, is a misnomer. There can only be nuclear self-destruction.

While the essays in this collection make for heavy reading, they will evoke somber reflection. And they reveal, in ways that Hartman's previously published writings do not reveal, the intimate connection between his witnessing of world history through the wars of the 20th Century and his development of the value theory known as formal axiology. Ending war became Hartman's life work; formal axiology was the means by which he saw the way to a world of peace.

Writing in the first chapter of the edited volume, Forms of Value and Valuation, Hartman's widow, Rita, had this to say about her late husband's life work:

> "Bob was dreaming of a world of peace. Hitler's horrendous crimes colored his whole thinking, and he hoped to be influential in seeing to it that such a nightmare would never happen again. His Theory of Value was his answer to the challenge of a horror which only ended with the victory of the allies over Germany. Hopefully the Theory of Value contributes to the aim that it could never happen again."

The Hartman Institute offers these collected essays with the same intention that Rita expressed—that Hartman's ideas do not become lost to history.

These essays will surely be of interest to historians of world politics. But, they also deserve a contemporary audience. In fact, today's reader needs this message.

6

If you need convincing of this, read the 2020 Doomsday Clock Statement of the Bulletin of the Atomic Scientists. This organization was founded in 1945 by scientists from the University of Chicago who had helped develop the first atomic weapons during the Manhattan Project. In their annual report, published each year since 1947, the Bulletin announces the board's decision to move forward or backward the time of the Doomsday Clock.

Borrowing the metaphor of a 2-minute warning from American football, they write, "The last two minutes bring newfound vigilance and focus to participants and viewers alike. Every second matters." Accordingly, in 2020 "the world has entered into the realm of the two-minute warning, a period where danger is high and the margin of error low."

The 2020 Bulletin warns us that, "The world is sleepwalking its way through a new unstable nuclear landscape. The arms control boundaries that have helped prevent nuclear catastrophe for the last half century are being steadily dismantled." [1]

In short, Hartman's warnings in these concluding essays are even more relevant today than when he first issued them.

My hope is that, through this collection of essays, as well as others in the Axiology Studies Series, Hartman's thinking will continue to make a positive difference in the lives of hundreds of millions of people around the world. In spite of the many, many challenges facing us today, perhaps we can all rise to the challenge of peace by preserving, refining, embracing, and making value judgments related to international affairs in alignment with the theory of formal axiology.

CLIFFORD G. HURST
Editor

---

[1] To read the most current Bulletin in full, go to: https://thebulletin. org/doomsday-clock/current-time/

CHAPTER I

In War as in Peace— Teamwork

EDITOR'S NOTE

The first chapter selected for this anthology of Hartman's writings is also one of the earliest found in the Archives about the topic of war and peace—at least among those that were written in English. It is dated February 24, 1943, or about 15 months after the United States entered World War II. The accompanying text was the script of a radio address delivered by Hartman in Danville, IL on that date. At the time, Hartman was a teacher at Lake Forest Academy in Lake Forest, Illinois.

Because it was written to be read aloud, this essay has an easy cadence to follow. Try reading it aloud or sub-vocalizing it as you read. But, be warned… its ease of comprehension will not mask the horrors of World War II that Hartman speaks about.

In spite of the evils that Hartman describes here, he ends on an optimistic note. He expresses here his hope that the world will long remember the crimes of conscience that allowed Hitler to rise to power in the first place and, thus, never repeat them.

The history of the world up to this moment has been a history of battles. It has been written in the blood of the common people, simple men and women without evil in their hearts, without desire for war, who have fallen, regularly and periodically, victims to the so-called strong men of history, those lords and leaders whom we still are accustomed to call "the great men." What was the method that enabled the strong throughout history to take advantage of the weak? What was the failure of the weak to let themselves be plunged, again and again, into the holocaust or war?

Whether we regard it as our opportunity or our calamity, we live in the most intensely and extensely historical period of all times. All past history has come to a culmination in our days: the past history of blood and battles culminates today in the holocaust of World War II. The history of individual peoples culminates in the present bloody experiences of all people on earth; the history of so-called "great men," culminates in the global horror of that one man, Adolf Hitler; and the history of weapons culminates in the fiendish super-weapon, the robot bomb.

Never has there been a man who in his own person has incarnated the evils of the historical conqueror in such crystal clearness as has Adolf Hitler. Never have the masses been seduced more alluringly, never have they been smashed more crushingly. What was Hitler's method? It was the old tested historical method of those who want to rule: *divide et impers*, divide and conquer. Good men divided are the steppingstones for the bad. Divide and conquer—that was Hitler's method, as it has always been the method of the wicked. Never has a generation had a more intense visual education in the methods of power than our generation. Step by step we would follow Hitler as he divided his enemies: the men and women of Munich, of Bavaria, or Germany, of Europe and finally, of the whole world. He sowed hatred among men; hatred of race, of profession, of class, of religion, hatred of parents against children, of man against wife, of brother against sister—like the devil, Mephistopheles himself, sowing discord and creating chaos throughout mankind.

What was the failure of the common people that they fell victim to this trick? Their main failure was not to see the trickery, not to see the devilish power, to let themselves be divided, to let themselves be conquered, to let themselves be ruled. Their failure was their cowardice

11

in front of the facts, their shortsightedness for and ignorance of the conditions of peace, their frantic endeavor to avoid responsibility. That is why the German parties, though theoretically against Hitler, through their indecision helped him to the triumph of the Wilhelmstrasse; why the nations of Europe, though theoretically against Hitler , through their cowardice helped him to the triumph of Munich; why the nations of the world, though theoretically against Hitler, through their neutrality helped him to the triumph of Compiègne.

Slowly, very slowly, did the conscience, the con-science, the "together-knowledge" of the world awake. It did not exist when Manchuria and Ethiopia were sacrificed. It did not exist when Czechoslovakia was betrayed. It did not exist when Scandinavia, Belgium, Holland, and Luxembourg, the so-called Oslo powers, refused to unite, it did not exist when these same countries looked at the "phony war", it did not exist when the United States sold to every customer that could pay when Poland or Russia made their treaties with Hitler.

Slowly, very slowly the conscience of the world awakened; slowly, very slowly, awakened their compassion with the victims of Hitler's aggressions. I myself saw with my own eyes how Czechoslovakian Jews and other pitiful refugees of Hitler's terror were seized by strong British policemen and shoved back into the planes they had just landed in, the planes ordered back to Prague and its passengers condemned to the death in Hitler's extermination camps.

With a little compassion, with a little conscience, with a little responsibility of all for all men on this globe, the whole catastrophe would have been avoided. Against the motto of the strong, Divide and Rule, the weak, the common people of the earth, you and I, must put the motto: Teamwork, in war as in peace—teamwork. Teamwork of all races, teamwork of all religions, of all classes, of all professions, teamwork of all families, teamwork of all nations.

This motto of Brotherhood is as old as history; it was written down in the immortal words of the testaments: Love thy neighbor as thou lovest thyself. These words were written down 4,000 years ago, in the Book of Leviticus; they were repeated and glorified for the whole world in the commands of Christ. History has never taken these words seriously; mankind has treated them as luxuries which we were free to take or to leave. Today these words must be followed. Today they are not luxuries, they are necessities. Today we either love our neighbor—or we perish. In the age of the robot bomb there is a death penalty on callousness and moral negligence. The globe has shrunk to a little planet, where every man can visit every other man within 60 hours, communicate with him in a flash, by telephone or radio; and be seen bodily by television in all countries. Man is actually bodily and mentally omni-present.

But while every man on earth thus is our neighbor, we still make reservations and regard this Jew over there as someone foreign, this African American over there as someone repulsive, this Chinese over there as someone strange, and this Mexican over there as someone lower. While our minds and bodies are spanning the whole earth, our soul, our power of compassion and conscience, is still provincial, nay, local. The power of radio transmissions and receptions is increased the further they have to reach, but the power of our compassion decreases geometrically with our distance from misery, the power of our sympathy even shrinks from our next-door neighbor. Yet, as this war proves, evil committed in a village in Manchuria is a crime against all mankind, including you and me. Because we neglected evil in the world, we are now suffering under evil in the world; because our responsibilities would not be global, now our sorrows are. For evil is as dangerous as a bacillus which, when not checked, can ravage humanity in devastating epidemics. As infantile paralysis starts with a cold, cancer with a mole, plague with a pimple—so evil starts with an innocent remark here, an innocent observation there. The gossiper and rumormonger, the jealous and envious man, the greedy and narrowminded, the vulgar and uncontrolled—avoid him as you do a man ridden with plague. He is the bearer of that bacillus that is now destroying the earth, the bacillus of hate. We all have some of it in us, we all have heard, if not actually said, words like "nigger' or "kike"—but remember, whenever we use such words, whenever we hear them and tolerate their use, we sow the seeds of death for our children in the next war! The pimple of evil, the little mole on the soul, the germ of evil; let us eradicate them from our hearts and minds, our thoughts and words and actions.

Right now, the germ is rampant and the epidemic is on. Has there ever been a statesman that has made 1600 million people miserable, eaten the strength out of their muscles, the marrow out of their bones, shriveled their bodies to skeletons, as do the famines and plagues that now ravage Europe, China and India? Has there ever been a germ that has exposed people to more ghastly deaths than the one men, women, and children are enduring today—packed in freight cars spread with lime that eat their naked bodies and suffocates them; packed into death cells where boiling steam makes them into one slimy mass; packed into churches and synagogues spread with gasoline where they burn to death; thrown alive into furnaces; impaled, tortured, flogged and flayed to death—evil is rampant; technological cannibals have gone mad with sadism—little people of Bavaria and Prussia, Wurttenberg and Lippe and Pomerania—the boys I went to school with gone mad with insanity—the insanity that starts with prejudice. They are infected with the germ of evil, evil grown into a gigantic epidemic, evil that grew up visibly before our eyes, in a few men. They were not checked, and today, like a plague, they take millions into the grave with them before we can get rid of them.

We could not check this plague in its beginning because we did not recognize it—just as we cannot yet check infantile paralysis because we do not yet know it. Yet, the principles are given to us to recognize evil—in our holy scriptures, in the laws of brotherhood; Love thy neighbor—have compassion with suffering man wherever he may be, and never think that his suffering is not your concern. It is your concern as vitally as if your neighbor were smitten with plague. He is smitten with evil, and evil will strike you unless you check it. Unless you check it. For unlike plague and paralysis the fight against evil cannot be left to the specialist in his laboratory. It has to be fought by every man in his own heart.

Thus, it is up to us to make this world a better place to live after this war. If we understand that to the global science of this age belongs a global power of compassion, that the power of technology today has to be matched by the power of religious consciousness—then we have grasped the secret of this time and age. Then among us there will arise the great leader of the new age, a leader not toward new battles nor toward new scientific discoveries, toward new means of harnessing the physical nature of man or the universe, but a leader toward discoveries of the soul, toward the discovery of those spiritual energies which are more powerful, more gigantic, more devastating and more blissful than any physical or scientific power. Then we shall be able to harness the powers of human nature and liberate man, turning passion into compassion, science into conscience, and fulfilling the prophecy of the Scriptures, that after the days of tribulation will come an age of the spirit. Perhaps it is our generation that shall not pass till all these things be done. Perhaps it is our generation that is to lead mankind, strong in mind and strong in soul, on the road to peace—the peace of the prophet and the Christian, mindful of evil, guarding the well-being of his fellow-man, and ever prepared to combat any force that touches his body, mind, or soul.

CHAPTER II
How to Win the Peace

EDITOR'S NOTE

Sol Bloom served as a member of the U.S. House of Representatives from New York starting in 1923 until his death in 1949. Bloom served as chair of the House of Representatives' Committee on Foreign Affairs beginning in 1938 and remained chair until his passing. These were critical years in U.S. foreign policy.

Bloom's own part in this chapter of U.S. history is told in The Autobiography of Sol Bloom (1948). It is from Bloom's autobiography that we can find a few scant details of the circumstances that prompted this next piece by Robert Hartman.

In the manuscript found at the Hartman archives, the memorandum entitled "How to Win the Peace" was written and submitted "at the request of Congressman Sol Bloom, Chairman of the Foreign Affairs Committee of the House of Representatives."

It is dated September 19, 1943. Let's provide some context for that date.

Bloom recollects a series of conversations he had during the first two years of WWII with other Congressmen, U. S. leaders, and even Winston Churchill about the "problems of war and peace." By the spring of 1943, the Allies had grown confident that they would win the war and therefore, must begin preparing for the peace. These discussions led to what became known as the Fulbright Resolution. The Resolution read:

> Resolved by the House of Representatives that the Congress hereby expresses itself as favoring the creation of appropriate international machinery with power adequate to establish and to maintain a just and lasting peace, among the nations of the world, and as favoring participation of the United States therein. (Bloom, p. 265).

Congress recessed for the summer with that resolution still pending. When Congress reconvened in September, the House passed the Fulbright Resolution by a vote of 360 to 29. The House then sent

the Resolution to the Senate. Meanwhile, the Senate had passed a very similar Resolution, known as the Connally Resolution.
On September 8, 1943, Italy surrendered to the Allies. Bloom writes, "After that there was always the feeling that we were now concerned not only with winning the war but with building a world of peace." (p. 267)

The Connally and Fulbright Resolutions were adopted by both houses of Congress shortly after that.

Bloom also describes that it was in the fall of 1943 that the United Nations Relief and Rehabilitation Administration (NRRA) was established. Treatment of refugees and displaced persons were issues of great interest to both Bloom and Hartman, as Hartman detailed in the chapter in this book recalling his "Report from Europe".

It was in this context of events that were very much on the minds of leaders of Congress that Hartman's memorandum "How to Win the Peace" was submitted. Hartman's ideas were very much in alignment, it seems, with the thinking of Sol Bloom himself, and also with the eventual steps the United States took regarding the immediate post-war years... the chartering of the United Nations, the Marshall Plan for reconstruction, and the transfer of the UNRRA under the auspices of the United Nations.

There's one thing I find perplexing about this memorandum by Hartman. How did a Spanish teacher at a private school in Illinois, who had immigrated to the U.S. less than two years before, come to be known to the Chair of the House Committee on Foreign Affairs and to be someone from whom the Chair of that committee sought advice?

We have not yet uncovered an answer during our search of the Archives, nor by reading of Bloom's autobiography. My own tentative conclusion is that Hartman and his ideas about international relations must have been more widely known in his own time than they are understood today by students and scholars of Hartman's life and work. Clearly, Hartman was no mere academic; he wanted his ideas known and put to use in the "real" world.

The peace after the last World War was not lost because of the Treaty of Versailles, or Hitler's dynamism, or any active force at all. It was lost due to passivity, to weakness rather than wickedness. Citizens seeing a fire starting and instead of extinguishing it quietly going about their business must not be astonished if the flames engulf them. They must not blame the fire but themselves. Of course, such an unconcerned attitude is almost unimaginable. Yet just such unconcern is the reason why we lost the peace.

While men have learnt to join forces and fight the elements of nature, they have not yet learned to join forces and fight the elements of evil. Yet, the forces of evil are essentially the same as the primitive elements of nature: mechanical forces trying to reduce men to mechanical things.

The ruthless elements of nature occasionally appear in the shape of men. Goethe knew this long ago when he called Napoleon one of the men who "step over the border of morality. They act finally like physical elements, like fire and water." He also knew that such forces cannot be appeased. Has it been forgotten all together that time gets value only through the activity of man? What are water and fire when we let them go on because of our stupidity, impotence, and carelessness?" They are scourges of mankind, just as are bacteria if they are not recognized and stopped, and as evil if it is not recognized and stopped.

The evil that arose in the man Hitler was neither recognized nor stopped. His success is due to a universal ignorance of the conditions of peace, a global inertia. We did not possess the consciousness of evil, let alone the will and power to crush it. We had no standards of good and evil, in spite of all our knowledge and philosophy. Otherwise we would have known Kant's categorical imperative, that evil exists wherever men are treated like things, and recognized Hitler as such a force trying to reduce men to things. We would have had the consciousness of evil, and probably the conscience to do away with it. We did not know that evil anywhere concerns everyone on earth, and that distances of lands and oceans are barriers against the spread of evil as little as against the spread of bacteria. Ours was a time without dignity and without conscience.

It is not necessary here to trace the infamous events that brought into focus this global inertia, the indecision of the Versailles peacemakers, the Japanese attack on Manchuria, Italy's attack on Ethiopia, the Geneva haggling over article 16 of the League's Covenant, Hitler's persecution of the Jews, his march into the Rhineland, the rape of Austria, the shame of Munich. In every one of these cases the flame of evil could have been quenched with relatively small force, but the intelligence of the world was not up to the occasion. Manchuria, Ethiopia, "did not concern us." Now this very same flame licks at our own house and our sons, brothers, and fathers die in it; and their graves are in stranger places, among Botocudes and Papuans, Bedouins and Eskimos. Our responsibilities could not be global, now our sorrows are.

Through ignorance and inertia we lost the peace; through ignorance and inertia we would lose the next one—and therewith perhaps our national freedom for ever. The next peace must be won; it cannot merely be maintained.

THE WORLD AFTER THE WAR

The world after the war will consist of two sections, one of which is to be shaped by us, the other to exist independent of our wishes. The first is the world of our present enemies, the second the world of our present friends, the United Nations.

Peace, as Litvinov has said, is indivisible, and a world with eternally hostile sections would not be a peaceful world. Our aim must be to convert our enemies into friends, and to prevent our friends from becoming enemies.

The Enemy World

Our dealing with the Enemy world must have a twofold aim: as long as they are enemies, we must prevent their becoming politically and militarily powerful again; as soon as they are friends we must treat them as we do all the other friendly nations.

How long are Germany and Japan to be regarded our Enemies?

We have declared that the war will not end unless Germany and Japan have capitulated unconditionally. In the case of Germany, we have specified that we would not deal with any Nazi government. In the case of Japan we have not made such a condition concerning the Mikado's government; on the contrary, we expect a peace offer from just that government and are very careful at the moment not to hurt the feelings of the Japanese for their Mikado or to touch with bombs the Imperial

Residence. While thus we disapprove of Germany's present Government and political institutions, we seem to approve of those of Japan. While Germany would be our enemy as long as the Nazi regime exists, the existence of the Mikado regime does not seem to be an obstacle to our peace and friendship with Japan. While we see in the German political system the root of war, in the case of Japan we have no such misgivings. Though we were attacked by Japan and not by Germany, and though the first attack in the post-Versailles world was made by Japan, we regard the Japanese form of government as less obnoxious than the German. This is a mistake which can have fatal consequences. What is true for Germany is in an even higher degree true for Japan. Both are our enemies as long as their present political systems exist.

Germany

It is true that Hitler has raped the German nation as he has the other nations under his power. It is true that he came to power through the inertia rather than the active participation of the German people. As little as anybody else did the Germans recognize the evil that was Hitler, and just as the Western Powers helped him to the triumph of Munich did the German nation help him to the triumph of the Wilhemstrasse. After the elections of 1932 Hitler, as the leader of the strongest party in the Reichstag, was automatically and within the mechanism of German democracy destined to become Chancellor of the Reich, a position he obtained in January 1933. Only gradually did the German nation awake to the evil of Hitler—just as the other powers only gradually awakened to it, some when it was too late, and this country only after Hitler's ally had attacked her. On the other hand it is true that Hitlerism in Germany is largely a condition of mind prevalent in wide ranks of the German people and anchored in the very depth of the German "soul." Heine, Verdi, and others have foreseen the eruption of German "Gemuet" and philosophy in a terrible cataclysm and seen in Fichte, Schopenhauer, Wagner, Nietzsche ideological archetypes of the coming catastrophe. Thus, while on the one hand the Germans were overwhelmed by the power of Hitlerism on the other hand this power arose from the very depth of their own nation, and it must be eradicated from it. A simple change of Government will not change the German mentality. A deeper going action is necessary.

After the last war German schoolchildren and the Germans at large learned that the war had not really been lost by Germany or won by the Allies. Dark powers within Germany herself—Jews, Jesuits, and Socialists—had stabbed the German armies in the back and thus brought about the collapse of the Kaiser's empire. This falsification of history was believed throughout Germany not only because it touched certain mythical strings of the German soul—the death of the fair hero Siegfried by the treacherous Hagen—but also because Germany had not really suffered in the last war and, with the exception of some food shortage, had not noticed it otherwise than in Headquarters bulletins. For four years therefore the war was victorious, the hero withstood gloriously the whole world, and the collapse was too sudden to be explained rationally. This time Germany is suffering, the war is right in their country, and an historical lie as last time will be impossible. The Germans are now learning that Hitlerism was a bluff, that they were duped by foul promises and that the entire direction of German politics was disastrous for Germany herself. The more bombs rain on Germany the more will the German soul be purified and matured for the tasks of peace. The surest means therefore to win the peace against Germany is to win the war in a most thorough manner.

It may be that the Nazis will install a fake-anti-Nazi government in order to sue for peace. Before accepting Germany's unconditional surrender we must make sure that Nazism is indeed dead, crushed by the rage of the German people itself. We must not accept a German Badoglio, as little as we should have accepted an Italian Badoglio. Only a revolution can bring Germany back to democracy, as only a revolution can bring Italy back to democracy. Our desire to fight the war must never be hindered by our desire to fight the European revolution. The revolution is on in Europe, and if it is not directed by the democracies it will be directed against them. Just as peace is indivisible so is Democracy. Only world-wide democracy can guarantee world-wide peace. Democracy is today the strongest power in Europe. Let us help her and not be deterred by the spectre of "chaos" or the fall of antiquated idols like miniature kings, or other feudal residues. The common man of Europe is on the march, and he will either march with us or against us. Whether or not we want it, we are chosen to fight the revolutionary war of the Twentieth Century, to make universal the ideals of our own revolution of 1776. If we betray our own ideals we will fail in the peace even if victorious in the war, and the torch of liberty will be taken out of our wavering hands and carried forward by the men of Europe. A sure way to lose the peace right now is the policy of expediency, the policy of Darlanism and Badoglio blunder. It is the policy of passivity that sanctions the evil because it is more practical at the moment. In the long run it will be disastrous, and the blood of our children will pay for our own saved skins.

Germany will be our enemy as long as the German people themselves have not crushed the powers of Nazism.

Japan

What is true for Germany is in even higher degree true for Japan. The strength of Japan is the unconditional belief in the divinity of the Mikado. No matter what actual power is wielded by the Mikado, his mere existence gives the Japanese people its strength. If evil is existing in Germany under Hitler, the system of unconditional subjection is even more pronounced in Japan, and men used as things even more radically, women being sold like cattle and the thought-control and mechanization of life more thoroughgoing. If we believe in indivisible peace and indivisible democracy, then there is no place for the Mikado in the world of democracy. Our war aim in Japan should be Japanese democracy— the downfall of the Mikado and all the undemocratic, antidemocratic institutions he stands for, even if he personally should be a likeable gentleman. What we have to destroy is not the man but the institution. The means to achieve this are again Allied bombs, bombs over Tokyo and bombs over the Imperial Palace. The superstitious mind of the Japanese will see in the destruction of the Mikado and his abode not a signal for further fanatical resistance in the name of the Mikado but a sign from heaven that the Western God is mightier than the Mikado. But even if they would be spurred to a new pitch of fanaticism we should not be deterred. We must not fight this war in the easiest but in the most effective way.

With the destruction of the Mikado—either from outside or from inside—the very fundament of Japanese nationhood would be destroyed and the collapse of the entire artificial Japanese system would follow. In the void that will then exist we will have to infuse our ideas of democracy, of the worth of every man and woman. On the other hand, if we leave the Mikado in power we will within another generation have the revenge war of a new powerful Japanese Empire, a war that might unite us against the newly awakened peoples of Asia in an immense flood.

Japan will be our enemy as long as a Mikado rules.

How are Germany and Japan to be treated? Provided that we finish the war as outlined anything we will do after the war with Germany and Japan will lead them back into the society of democratic nations. On the other hand, if we do not so terminate the war, accepting either a Nazi, Junkers, or Army fake-government in Germany or leaving in power the Mikado in Japan, anything we will do after the war with Germany and Japan will help them to become our most powerful and revengeful enemies again. Any other means, occupation, disarmament, de-industrialization, dismemberment, will only be surface actions, ineffective in the long run unless the mentality is changed and the spirit of aggression fostered by the institutions of Nazism and Shintoism broken. The following outline applies only to a Germany and Japan thus definitely and thoroughly beaten and stripped of their undemocratic institutions. Any other termination of the war would be futile.

After the end of hostilities "chaos" will rule, and have to rule, in the beaten countries. This "chaos," so dreaded by us, is the ferment out of which will yeast the future. In this period of chaos, the transition period from totalitarian to democratic power, from enemy to friendly nation, we have to assist to make sure that the growth will indeed be one that will fit into the democratic flora of the world. We will have to occupy and rule these two countries. Our occupation will have to have a twofold aim: to wind up the war and to prepare the future.

The Government of Occupation in the first phase will have to relieve the material needs of the population, to administer the territories and bring them back to normal life, and to reconstruct what was destroyed. During this period, which may last for several years, no independent political life will be allowed in the territories. They are not yet our friends nor are they our enemies. They are protectorates which we have taken over in order to make them independent at a time when we see that they have grown up. However, during this period we shall foster all the elements and political or ecclesiastical movements in the country that attempt to establish democratic institutions and infuse democratic spirit into them. One of the main tasks and one that most definitely and essentially will prepare these countries for their future democratic role will be supervision and direction of their educational system.

In the case of Japan this task may well be left to the Chinese, who already 1300 years ago brought to the Japanese barbarians their superior culture, in the Taikwa period of "Great Civilization." That culture kept Japan on the path of relative peace and righteousness until the Shinto restoration, the Isshin period of 1868 and the adoption of Western technology. Such a Chinese re-education of Japan, in the old spirit of Emperor Kotoku and of Chinese wisdom, would be mutually beneficial to both China and Japan. Japan would profit as it would again be given a chance to attach itself to the cultural heritage of Asia which it has almost lost. China on the other hand would learn the technological skills which the Japanese have acquired, and which China needs as bitterly as Japan needs China's political and spiritual sagacity. White men's activities in Japan should not be predominant, and mainly consist in those of the administrators who have to care for the material needs and industrial and military supervision of Japan, and those of the Christian missionaries, actively aided by the United Nations governments. The spiritual renaissance of Japan should be left to the Chinese scholar and the Christian missionary.

In the case of Germany we have an outstanding opportunity of preparing the democratic and cultural foundations for a lasting democracy. In this country, as all over the United Nations, the great German scholars, authors, teachers, are living as refugees. The re-education of Germany should be started immediately by forming a Council for the Democratic Education of Germany, members of which should be the leading refugees, with Thomas Mann and Albert Einstein at the head, and the many democratic Germans, teaching in this country and in England and other parts of the world as members. This Council should prepare the curricula of German schools, universities, prepare text-books, and be ready to follow the conquering armies and set up a German Educational Organization together with the Government of Occupation. This is one of the most essential, if not the most essential task for winning the peace with Germany. According to a communication received by the undersigned from the State Department on March 24, 1943, nothing has been done yet in this respect.

When the conquered territories have returned to normal life and the democratic powers in them grown up, the second phase of the post-war period will begin, the graduation of the former enemy nations from the course in applied democracy to democratic self-government. General elections will be held, on a completely democratic basis, in order to convoke a National Assembly that will outline the New Constitution of the country and install the first National Government. The Government of Occupation will continue as an advisory body until the political system of the country is consolidated. It will only withdraw when it is sure that a vigorous democracy is functioning in the territories.

The entire period from the end of hostilities to the withdrawal of the Occupation Forces will be covered by the terms of an Armistice. Only when the Occupation Forces withdraw will the terms of Peace be negotiated between the autonomous governments of the United Nations and those of the former Enemies. The object of the Peace should be the integration of the former Enemy Nations in the world of the United Nations.

THE WORLD OF THE UNITED NATIONS

The example of Finland and Italy has taught us how fast friends can become enemies and enemies, friends. Our post-war policy toward our Allies must be to keep them as our friends.

The world of the United Nations will consist of the four large sections of America, the British Commonwealth, Russia, and China. Both peace and democracy being indivisible we must endeavor to keep up the organization of the United Nations for common action in peace and, if necessary, war. However, if the conquered nations are being treated as outlined, they will be unable and unwilling to ever become again enemies of democratic nations. While therefore the United Nations will have to cooperate during the first phase of the Armistice in bringing the conquered nations back into the society of democracies, they will have to work in the following Peace as members of a world where the old friend-enemy divisions have disappeared and all have to cooperate that none will appear again. In that second phase every one of them will have to work for Democracy at home as well as abroad.

The First Phase

During the first phase the United Nations will have a common concrete task: administering the conquered territories and preparing them for peace. The peace will be lost at once if the United Nations cannot agree on the manner of treating the conquered nations after the war. If, for instance, the views of Russia and England diverge concerning Germany, or the views of China and the United States concerning Japan, both Germany and Japan will be able to play out the one against the other, and the old game of power politics with its certainty of another war will be on again. An absolutely indispensable condition of the next peace is the agreement of the United Nations concerning the treatment of conquered territories.

Provided that such an agreement has been reached the United Nations would continue to function as common trust-holders of the conquered territories and administer them in a common spirit. In that phase there is no necessity of another formal bond between them.

The Second Phase

The Peace negotiations, however, must find the United Nations as a unity not for a specific concrete aim, as the administration of territories, but with a common ideal for the preservation of world peace and an organization to guarantee the realization of this idea.

Believing in democracy as we do and educating the conquered nations to the ideals of democracy as we intend to, we presuppose as a matter of course the adherence of the United Nations themselves to democracy. The war will have sharpened our eyes for the evil that spells war, and wherever whenever it turns up again, whether in our own midst, within our allied friends' territories, or in neutral countries, we must recognize it as a potential source for losing the peace again. Thus, if races or religions or personal freedom at large are persecuted in any territory, we must make such persecution our own affair and try to eradicate it as a potential source of war. There should be created an office for the Protection of Minorities, an Office for Minorities, as an active agency of the United Nations. This office should have field agencies throughout the United Nations territory, as well as in the territory of other nations who would like to join. The main purpose of these agencies should be the observation of ethical trends—just as we have observation posts for meteorological or geological, economic or sociological movements. Wherever persecution of race, religion, or personal freedom appears, if in an ever so small degree, it should be regarded as a manifestation of that unconquered part of human nature that brought about the war. It should be registered, as seismographs register even the finest motions of the earth, and its strength be measured according to the number of participants and the intensity of the action. Thus a lynching committed by fifty people should have a certain index number, and the antisemitic remark of a housewife—a punishable offence in certain countries—another. In this way an organization can be set up that will keep track of the most perilous of all natural currents and plot its course from day to day and town to town. Though it will not interfere in the personal freedom of anyone it will through its very existence, make mankind conscious of these trends and thus help her to combat them. It would be an office of ethical statistics and prognostication.

Such an organization would perform another service. It would test the seriousness of every partner in the United Nations' society, as Russian sincerity in democracy, England's or Holland's sincerity in their colonies, and so on. The key observers, as all the key officials of the United Nations as such, should be men with responsibility to the United Nations alone and under no other jurisdiction but that of the United Nations.

This presupposes the creation of a United Nations Court and judicial system, to be established and defined by the Peace Treaty.

Finally there will have to be a United Nations Police Force, a standing Army, Navy, and Air Force under the command and at the disposal of the United Nations' combined General Staff. Since, through the agency of the Minority office—which may also be called the War Prevention Office—the trends leading to war will be scientifically plotted, the stationing of this Force can be undertaken with wide foresight. The "outbreak" of a war will then be very improbable, should it, however, occur, whether through the attack of a United Nation or a neutral country, the Force would be moved quickly and without compromise. It should be avoided as far as possible to have members of this Force stationed in their own home territory. This and other questions concerning the composition and functions of the International Force have to be regulated through the Peace Treaty.

With a Minority Office, a United Nations Court, and a United Nations Police Force established as fundamental institutions to be complemented by other agencies mainly of an economical nature—the integration of the former enemy nations into this United Nations world will not be too difficult.

THE ORGANIZATION OF THE PEACE

Peace negotiations will not begin before the enemy nations have converted themselves democratically to such a degree as to possess their own democratic governments. They will then be in a position to be admitted into the ranks of the United Nations, which will thus expand into an organization comprehending practically the whole world. The Peace Treaty will thus be the founding Covenant of a new League, a League with sharp organs of discrimination and powerful organs of execution.

The much debated question of the territorial boundaries of the former enemy nations will then lose its predominant importance. During the first phase of occupation the territories will be divided into sections convenient for their efficient administration. During this period Germany or Japan will not exist as such, but as "occupied territories," administered by the United Nations according to United Nations principles. Only when these territories are to be handed over to autonomous governments does the question of their boundaries arise—but then these countries will be democratic and thus again the question will lose its vital importance.

Immediately after cessation of hostilities all territories conquered by Germany and Japan will be restored to their rightful owner, the United Nation in question. Thus during the first phase the pre-war divisions will exist, all the small countries of Europe will again be in existence, and the Netherland Indies returned to the Netherlands and French Indo-China to France. But this will only be a provisory state of affairs, to be revised and definitely determined at the Peace Table. At that time, together with the agencies, armies, and institutions of the United Nations also their boundaries will be established.

Since all the United Nations are members of a world-wide effective organization the notion of national sovereignty will have to undergo a drastic change and true sovereignty be reserved for the organization itself, the member nations being administrative rather than sovereign bodies, each of them allowing the over-all organization certain deep-going influences in its territory. The importance of territorial boundaries and territorial rule is thus greatly diminished. There is then no reason why not every population, in the United Nations' territory as far as its status had been changed during the war and in the conquered territories at large, should not choose its own form of administration. Germany, stripped of her war-conquests may well be left to decide at the Constitutional Election or some other occasion whether it wants as a whole to belong to the United Nations or whether the individual states, Bavaria, Prussia, etc. would prefer to belong to them directly. Germany having gone through the inferno of war and the educational period of the Armistice will be no worse candidate for democratic behavior in the post-war world, subject to United Nations organizational principles, than any other nation. Thus, if Germany as a whole wanted to be a member state of the United Nations, it should be acceptable. A forced dismemberment of Germany would make her unfit of becoming a partner in the United Nations' society, a society which is a voluntary association of free nations, and turn her not toward world cooperation but again toward German unity in opposition to the world. Also the problems of Austria, of the Danubian, Eastern European, or Scandinavian Confederations would then find their natural solutions. The United Nations would accept big and small states alike, Germany as well as Luxembourg, Hungary as well as a "Danubian Confederation." The outer size of a state will be a criterium for admission to the United Nations as little as in the United States of America, where tiny Rhode Island exists peacefully and with equal rights beside huge Texas. Even if the whole of Europe should want to combine into one state, "The United States of Europe," the United Nations would receive such a state within their ranks. As long as there is a firm supra-national, global organization, administrative and territorial changes within the affiliated or subordinated territories concern the Whole as little as would the corporation or separation of individual states within the United States, as long as these states adhere to the principles of the Union. But if the United Nations' organization is weak in power and principles, then no activity of any of its present or future member nations will be sufficient to prevent the next world catastrophe.

CHAPTER III
The Triumph of Gravitation

EDITOR'S NOTE

In 1943, at the height of U.S. involvement in World War II, and approximately two years after Hartman immigrated to the United States from Mexico, he completed a monumental manuscript about the spiritual causes of war. He entitled it "On God's Side." It was monumental both in its scope and its length—850 manuscript pages.

Hartman wrote "On God's Side" as an extended dialogue between himself and his deceased father who, having died ten years before, could see the travails of humanity during WWII from God's perspective. It is a mind-bending manuscript, unlike any of Hartman's published writings, which tend to be intellectual, analytical, logical, and, dare I say it, dry? Not "On God's Side." It is written metaphorically, which as Hartman would later in his life describe, is the language of the intrinsic.

So, we include in this collected volume of Hartman's writings on war and peace an excerpt from an early chapter of "On God's Side," a chapter he entitled, "The Triumph of Gravitation." Here, Hartman metaphorically equates war with the power of gravity—a force pulling mankind, pulling the landscape into a great leveling down, into a quagmire from which we must rise again. He continues with a second metaphor, that of the soldiers of the totalitarian state being robots and of soldiers from free states—in particular, the United States—as soldiers of a different sort. Soldiers of independent free will. Soldiers as persons.

Hartman calls for victory of the free world over the totalitarian states of Germany and Japan. In fact, he declares that this must be a total victory—a declaration that, later in his life Hartman sees as no longer possible due to nuclear weapons. Remember, this was written in 1943, well before he had any knowledge of the development of the atomic bomb.

As you read this chapter, keep in mind the date at which it was written, the circumstances under which it was written, and the metaphorical style in which it was written.

The Hartman Institute is making plans to publish the entire manuscript of "On God's Side," from which this chapter is excerpted. If you are interested in supporting our efforts to publish that manuscript in its entirety, please visit the Institute's website to learn how you can help.

Dear Father:

This is my second war. When you were in the first, I was just a little boy, eight years old when you returned, with the bullet-hole through your helmet. Yes, I well remember how I welcomed you—one of the silly chapters of my life. Trying to become a martyr! Well, I don't think those ideas came to me only through reading books about the saints. I had heard so much about you in the war, I thought that maybe all of you were martyrs for the great cause of the world, and that I should like to do my share in the general martyrdom. I well remember when you came home and we had that conversation in the evening, when I asked you when you would go to the war again. And you said: "Never. It's peace." I still remember how bewildered I was by that new word. When the war began, I was just four, so the state of the world for me was war. Now you said that there was peace. I asked you: "What is peace?" and I still remember you looking at me in amazement and then looking into yourself in amazement, and then saying: "Peace—that is no war." Indeed, what else could you have said?

To me that made perfect sense, because I had my definite ideas about "war". "No war" for me was a well-paved street—which may not be such a bad symbol for "peace." War for me was a very definite thing. I had often heard the other children say that their father or brother or uncle had "fallen in the war." I didn't then distinguish very clearly between in and into, and figured war was a big hole, like the manholes in the streets, well-cemented inside, with those iron rungs like stairs leading to the depths of the hole. The trains with the soldiers—because I had seen many trains with soldiers—stopped at those holes, the soldiers stepped out, climbed down, and down there big fighting went on. A man who had fallen in the war was an unfortunate who by accident had fallen down the hole.

When today I remember that childish idea—and it is still so vivid in my mind that I almost think war is just such a hole—I am amazed how much sense it actually makes. Yes, indeed, war—that is the greater attraction to mother earth; war, that is men digging themselves into the folds of the earth, men clinging to the earth, men taking advantage of every bend of the landscape, men eyeing eagerly how best to protect themselves in a certain terrain in order to destroy most intensely the terrain close to where the enemy is. War—that is the great falling: men's final defeat by gravity.

And war is the great reversal, men living not in light but in darkness, not living and letting live but dying and killing, men returned into the primitive stage of crawling and preying animals—the whole story of evolution reversed, the wheel of creation turned back.

I know, the aim of all of it is to create new souls in the horror. But, to tell you the truth, I don't see how the new souls are created on the battlefield, how the robots who master the battle turn into children of God after it. Nature needs the battles of men in unbalanced times to balance her metabolism of life and death. She needs perfected souls in the desert of one-sided intellects—and isn't war in the last analysis the great battle? Shouldn't the great battle be the place where incomplete men are to be converted into men? Where souls are to be infused into the soulless and the height of suffering open the depths of human souls? Yet who triumphs on the battlefield but the robots? Who mounts his flag triumphantly but the great beast, the master of situations, the men whose supreme senses are the nostrils and whose iron monsters are willing tools of their robot-minds? We have seen how men can become robots, and I can see how they triumph in their supreme achievement, war. But I cannot yet see how nature can gain in the bloody turmoil and draw the souls from it.

War—the art of negative landscaping, indeed. The battle—the master-architect of annihilation. Look at a battlefield. There are the torsos of houses; mostly the chimneys remain, a forest of chimneys—

the absolute fireplace, as it were, the fireplace per se. Fire—the essence of war as of nations. The chimneys are the desolate symbols of utter destruction. Then there are the torsos of churches—mostly window-frames in a heap of ruins, with a larger heap where the spire was. All buildings have their particular way of being shaped by battles. There are the wooden houses: just blueprints remain of them, with the groundwork showing exactly where the kitchen was and bedroom and the stable. And the streets are mostly holes—indeed, the holes I saw as a child, and many others. The battle shapes them all in different ways, but with one fundamental design: to make them all alike, create the greatest possible sameness. It is the Second Law in its pure form.

God divided the light from the darkness—the battlefield mixes them and grey smoke lies over it, obscuring the sun. He separated above from below—the battlefield mixes it all again. The dead that were buried now hang over the trees, and the living are buried dead. The earth, well-formed and furrowed below is not fine dust in the air and dirty patches over ruins. The air, to be breathed by men at the level of their heads, is buried underground and goes off with terrible explosions. The earth, the solid mass under our feet, flies into the sky, and the birds, that used to fly, fall down into the big holes. He separated water from land—the battlefield mixes them up again. The river is now a muddy paste, whirling along in a bloody mess of things, bodies, and dirt. And the earth, again, is a soaked mass, where men sink to their knees and remain there for the rest of their lives. He created trees, symbols of the ever branching creativeness of His being, diffusing themselves into the air, and, ever subdividing, separating limbs into branches, branches into twigs—the battlefield mixes them up again, tears the twigs from the branches, the branches from the limbs, and buries them in the muddy mass. The branchless trees of the battlefield—a few naked limbs stretched to the sky like despairing arms. He created grass, that the herb-yielding seek, the animals—and man, the crown of creation, made in His image—the battlefield mixes them all up. They are features in the sameness of the battered earth, the lifeless landscape; men become heaps of earth and grass grows in their corpses.

The earth is like one big wound. Landscaping is the cosmetics of the earth—war its laceration. It is a scientific laceration—a dissection with the cold passion of the perverted mind, like the politeness of

Mr. Goebbels. "We are polite to the last rung of the ladder," "Vengeance is a dish that has to be enjoyed cold". Yes, they enjoy it, the robots, their cold minds dissect the earth with glee and the hope of catching as many men in the dirt as possible. We have to learn that from them. Before our spirits can overcome them, we have to learn their big and little tricks. We have to become robots, too, in our actions, and still keep the flame of the spirit alive which will melt our steel when peace is won.

***

The problem is very simple. The enemies are cogs in a big machine that directs them, not men but robots. What we are fighting against are institutions gone mad. We, on the other side, are human beings, sorely unbalanced, mind-heavy and poor in soul. There are only two ways open to us. Either we go on as we were, and our minds will degenerate to the present state of our empty souls, or our souls will catch fire again, and our sufferings and defeats will turn us to the values of human existence and fill our souls with awe and enthusiasm, confidence and despair. We shall learn to believe—in the greatness of God, the humanity of man, the power of the spirit or however we wish to express it. Never mind the expression—believe! With the fullness of our souls the balance of our spirits will return, and with it our minds will become stronger, too. We shall, without knowing it, learn all the tricks of the enemies, all the cheap little, nasty, abominable products of their perverted robot-minds. But while their mind and craftiness and resourcefulness slowly but surely degenerate in the disequilibrium of their make-up, our keenness of mind, craftiness and resourcefulness will grow with every setback and every triumph. We shall be well-balanced men, of acute minds and inspired souls, and in that balance shall develop every side of man, even the side needed to overcome robots. I think it is as simple as that: learn to believe.

It may be that it is all the same to nature who wins this war. All she wants is new life, and death is her device. But no, nature needs the balance of the spirits just as we need it. Without that balance she would be unable to go on having life. If the wrong side won this war, the disequilibrium of men would leave nature without any developed souls at all. There would no longer be life but machines, robots ruling the lifeless globe. And that would be nature's own end—because the life of man is her achieved life. It would mean that she had been defeated by the systematic liars, by the systematic destroyers of all her purpose. It would mean the end of the universe—yes, the unimaginable end of all things. It would mean that the broom of the sorcerer's apprentice had triumphed, and that creation had slipped out of God's hands. All that can't be, just as little as two times two can be five. We know it—thus we believe, and God, man, and nature will have won when these hours of despair have passed.

It is an undignified undertaking we are engaged in. But you have taught me that no work is undignified, and everything has to be done that the day demands. You scolded me when I told you that I like to contemplate. Perhaps you thought I had better go and make some money for my family. You showed me how important it is to care about the material things of life as well as the spiritual—and to like them as well. Outwit the tricky, be shrewder than the shrewd and colder in purpose than the robots. Beat them at their own game and let the cold fear appear in them. To earn money is a certain enjoyment, a sort of triumph, a war whose trophy is the dollar. It is a crafty business, because the dollar was in another fellow's pockets before it came into my own. It is a complicated business, because the stream of monetary circulation has to be led through my account. And we enjoy that business and everything that goes with it, as long as it does not fill our entire personality. It is the same with that ghastly business of war. Just let us enjoy it, but don't let it absorb our personality. Let us remember that we are fighting for our belief in the good. And, with the help of God, we shall finish it as it must be finished.

Fortunately for us, God can't afford not to help us. He has developed man from crude beginnings in atoms and cells to the being that is potentially everything. Man is the great potentiality. He can be a tightrope dancer or a professor, a ventriloquist or a hairdresser, or all of these things. But the ants, the most highly developed social animals, are born into their roles, frozen in them. The totalitarian state freezes men in particular roles. Fullness of life may be enjoyed only by the ruler. The people are ants—and the soldier is man when he was still an experiment in the hand of God. The engineer is still the beaver, the dispatcher still the antelope, the scout still the giraffe, and the trench-digger still the mole. Their role is the entire content of their lives, and death in that role is the supreme achievement they are educated for. But the soldier in a free army is a better engineer than the totalitarian, a better dispatcher, a better scout and a better trench-digger. He knows everything the beaver, antelope, giraffe, and mole know, but he knows more. He is a man in the image of God and with the full powers of a man. He is not an animal in human shape, a robot, but a free man fighting for free men of his own will.

The soldiers of a totalitarian army are tools of their states, educated and trained for the particular tasks of war—including the last, death. The soldier of a democratic army is a free man, educated and trained for a particular profession in life. He is in a new role—but he hasn't given up his personality and individuality in it.

There are still great differences among the individuals of the democratic army. The army—and that holds true for the navy and air-force as well—is an individuated, well differentiated manifold. It is an orderly whole in the sense in which we have defined order in physical science. The army of the totalitarian state is a specialized whole, like the army of the democracies, but not individualized. There are no individualities in it, only different members executing different functions. It is a great monotonous pattern of sameness—of soldiers, not of men—and thus an unordered whole.

Beneath its sameness and monotony is the great fear, and once the armies of the democracies have outwitted the totalitarian armies and scratched off the thin layer of craftiness from the surface, they will encounter this fear. The totalitarian soldiers are homunculi in a phial, in the fog of their own propaganda of invincibility, working well as long as the world does not touch them with superiority. Let them feel our superiority, and the whole artificial product will evaporate and the phial burst.

The totalitarian state is interested only in the bodies of its soldiers—they are extended organs. Some are good at hearing and have the corresponding machines, sounding apparatus, airplane detectors; others are good at seeing, and have telescopes, periscopes and other-scopes; others are good at smelling, and sniff around with sniffing apparatus, such as gas-detectors and other things. Still others are good runners—they are extended feet, and have the corresponding machines, bicycles, motorcycles and cars. They are all personified senses—and as such they are very good. But a soldier is not only an appendage of a terrain, he is also an inhabitant of the earth and a part of the universe. The soldiers of the totalitarian powers never raise their spirit to those heights, they are senses, clinging to the terrain and the particular situation. Thus, they are masters of those situations, as long as the soldiers of democracy have not yet awoken to their great role. But once they have, those personified senses, those supreme bodies will be nothing. Nothing—namely absent, crossed out in the great account book of nature.

***

The robots are body-machines, and their strength and weakness ensue from it. Their weakness will appear as soon as spirit and belief appear on our side. They will have to appear everywhere, at home, where the machines are to be built, on the long way to the battlefield where they have to be tested along with our spirits. We always say that our spirits are fine, but we lack the machines. Well, we lack them because our spirits have not been fine. We did not see or did not want to see that finally the robots would turn against us, we were too slow and too late— we were too lazy. There is a song by Schubert, one of his most beautiful songs, about a lovely little trout, that darted through the water, and a bad fisherman lured it to its death. The poet of the song describes the trout and the bad fisherman, and how it finally dies, and he describes himself. "And I with lazy heart looked on, looked on." It's a beautiful song, and always when I hear or sing it I must think of the lazy hearts of those who look on, look on, until themselves are caught. When our soldiers and sailors fight with high spirits in desperate positions, we mustn't fool ourselves, it isn't our fine spirit. It is their individual spirit—and if our spirits had been better all the time these men wouldn't have to fight in desperate positions. With their individual gallantry they have to make good for all our many years of indolence. Thus, we need new spirits at home as well as on the front, new spirits all over wherever we have to see to it that the monsters are defeated.

It is indeed a fight against the dragon, a fight against the primitive lusts of men, a fight against nature reversed. The reversal is everywhere and in everything. We have to develop our souls in order to develop our minds instead of vice-versa. We have to go back into the jungles and the depths of the earth and sea and the heights of the air, whence we came when we were fishes, birds, and monkeys. Everything is reversed. The young die and the old live, children are taken from their parents, pigs are used as grenades and nature as the artificial, in camouflage. Books are buried in coal mines, pictures in bank vaults, and monuments are melted into bullets. At the height of the machine age, people have to ride bicycles because there are no tires, to ride in horse-drawn taxis because there is no gasoline or just to walk, if they have shoes. They have to starve because there is no bread and butter, and to die of epidemics because there are no medicines. Women are educated in all the refinements of sex in order to bear many soldiers, but the soldiers are to die and the children die of starvation. Bodies are sent by registered mail, and the glorification of the body in uniform is coupled with the mutilation of bodies in battles and concentration camps. It is all part of one great pattern of reversal. In millions of years man learnt to stand up and resist gravity on two legs, using his arms and hands for fine arts instead of for climbing trees. In war the entire evolution is turned back to the state not of monkeys, animals, or plants, who all triumph over gravity and stand up, but back to the stones—physical bodies. War is the triumph of gravitation.

***

We have learned now that man is a very tiny creature, but his spirit is very great. I know how dependent is the whole world and God Himself on what we do and neglect to do. Well, in America a great idea has been realized, and it may be that on its realization depends all the success or failure of God's creation. In America the idea that men are created in God's image has become truth. Men—that is all men, not just some. A country founded on that idea is a country whose citizens are privileged and obliged to develop all their energies, and talents to do good works. The American institutions are the institutions of free men. After this war they will be the institutions of free men all over the world. We are living in the greatest period of American history which, at the same time, is the greatest period in the history of the world. The world, hitherto an assembly of small provincial countries, will after this war for the first time in history consciously become what it always has been unconsciously: a unity, the home of mankind. It so happens that that new world will be an American world. It will be won by American blood, American sweat, American tears. It will be gained by American men, planes, arms, ships, tools.

***

It is a double task. First, we have to make the world safe for democracy. Then we have to make democracy safe for the world.

First, we have to win the war, and win it in such a way as to become the masters of the world. Then we have to become good masters. First, we have to crush the totalitarians. Before we can think of their spirit we must see to their right death. What we need in these hours is faith and determination.

We have spoken about our definite war aims: have the Japanese destroy their God Emperor, the Italians their Fascists, the Germans their Nazis. Let us remember, they have to do it themselves, and we have to inject them with bombs and fire until their soul awakes, and they do the dirty work. Don't let us do it ourselves! That would only be a half-measure. Don't let us make peace with any of those peoples unless they liberate themselves. Don't let us make peace with a caste within these peoples. The mass of Japanese, Germans, and Italians must do their job—not their armies, princes or other forces. This is an important point, and if we forget it the result will be another Versailles and another war in the next generation—that time perhaps the end of human life on earth. We mustn't make peace unless the German, Japanese and Italian masses revenge themselves for their slavery.

We mustn't make peace, even when things occur which we don't now foresee. Let us remember that we ourselves will have to suffer grimly. Don't let us succumb to our sufferings or slacken in our determination. Ours will be the victory. It is our blood, tears, sweat, and effort that have to win the new world. Nobody else can win it for us. We are the strength of our allies, but we mustn't rely on their being our strength. It is our world that is being fought for, and the fighting must be done by us. There will be many forces that will try to lure us into a cheap peace, that will try to exploit our suffering and weaken our determination. But we mustn't be lured. It is the Devil that will lure us, even if he appears in the shape of an old, dear, very good friend. If we let ourselves be lured the world will go to the Devil—and not the one who will be luring us. Well, we have spoken enough of how we will win the war: through suffering and determination—with clear aims.

When our generation has achieved such a definite victory, we will have accomplished half of our task. We will have made the world safe for democracy. Then we will have to make democracy safe for the world— that is the other half of the task. But that we shall to fulfill in the hearts and minds of our children. It is they who must earn the heritage our generation will confer on them, a heritage which has been conferred upon countless generations of Britons: the whole world. But the realm of the English will have been a province in comparison to the realm we will bequeath our descendants. There will be the British dominions, and Britain herself who will look to us for guidance. There will be the people of the Orient, the Indians, Chinese, and Japanese. There will be the nations of Europe. Only Russia will be a world in itself, but even Russia may look to us for advice—and vice versa, we to Russia.

Russia will be the country of the soul that will have developed its mind in new experiments, while we shall be the country of the mind that will have developed its soul in eternal beliefs. We shall be complementary.

All this, let me repeat it, only if we win the war as it will have to be won. Otherwise we will just be a small continent, locked in our own borders, and there will be other great empires who have never been promised the leadership of the world but who have usurped parts of it because we were too weak to stop them. There would be a Japanese Empire, comprising the whole Eastern Pacific and the mainland of Asia. There would be a German Empire, ruling the continent of Europe. There would probably be a very small Russia, and after some time a very small America. Because there is no room for Russia and America in a world of Japan and Germany, just as there is no place in a world of America and Russia for Japan and Germany. It is a fight to the end, and any compromise will lead to death. The victory of Japan and Germany would be the victory of the Devil, and the death of the world of God. It would be the definite failure of God's great career. It ought not be possible, but let me repeat, the new world will be won only through our suffering, determination, and clear aims.

Once we have thus won, a world will be ours comparing with the British Empire as the latter did to the Roman Empire. Yet ours will not be an empire, or even a dominion, but will consist in leadership. Let us remember this word and not confuse it with dominion or empire. Power is a dangerous thing, we know that, and we need all our strength of character to resist its temptations. America will survive in a long reign of leadership if she shows character.

***

44

And here is where our task comes in. Our children will not know from experience of the greatness and temptations, the glory and horror of our time. They will grow up in a time of peace, when all the past will seem to them as natural as their daily affairs. They will inherit a world which has just recovered from the exhaustion of war and begun a new flourishing epoch of human existence. They will grow up in a country that is the most powerful in that world, without that power being obvious in symbols and emblems all over the globe. They will have to know that the power of their country is not the force that lies in their weapons, soldiers, or any of their material riches, but that it was won through the spirit of their fathers when they used their arms. They must know that a nation in order to live and flourish must be powerful in spirit, and that their country will be great as long as its institutions live in their hearts. In a word: they must know that power comes to him who believes in the good, and that the good is the balance between mind and soul, body and spirit. They must know that all technical achievements are worth nothing if not coupled to achievements of the soul. They must know their soul.

CHAPTER IV
The Science of Peace

EDITOR'S NOTE

This essay, undated, appears to have been written circa 1948-1949. These were the years when Hartman taught at the College of Wooster. It is unclear whether Hartman's intent was to have the essay that comprises this chapter published in some journal or whether it was written as the foundation of a book to be written on the subject. We offer it here, as part of this collection, as a valuable contribution to the thoughts of a deep thinker as he wrestled with and through a lifetime concern about the subject of war and peace—as a matter of political practice, as well as a matter of morality and spirituality.

This is a complex and difficult-to-read chapter, but one well worth studying. In establishing a scientific framework by which the subject of peace can be studied, Hartman foreshadows his not-yet articulated theory of formal axiology.

After describing to the reader his understanding of the root causes of war, Hartman begins to lay out a theoretical foundation for a science of peace. In order to study the behavior of humankind scientifically, he sets forth the need for methods of abstraction, precision, situational analysis, and moral skills. Regarding the topic of precision, Hartman writes in this essay, "In order to research a phenomenon we need dimensions and standards by which to measure it." He argues for the development of a "situational Gestalt" and mentions in a footnote that this is the subject of a forthcoming book by him. It is unclear from the context what book Hartman is referring to. Perhaps it was never published; perhaps a manuscript to which he refers remains to be found in the Archives.

No mention is made in this essay using the terms either "axiology" or "formal axiology." Yet, there are plenty of pointers to that soon-to-be-articulated theory throughout. We can tell from the content that Hartman is getting close

to articulating this theory. In fact, in his autobiography,
Freedom to Live, *Hartman dates this development:*

*By the close of 1949 I was sure that formal axiology could be
the ordering logic for the value sciences. But my first writing
efforts to tell my colleagues about my discoveries and their potentialities failed to stir much enthusiasm. They were politely
interested but, as some told me, uncomprehending. Then came
the annual meeting May 3, 1951, of the American Philosophical Association at Evanston, Illinois. I was to give a
paper on "A Logical Definition of Value." ... Delivering my
talk, I had sensed first that my audience was unbelieving;
then, when they caught the gist, they became intrigued with
the unfolding of my system; and I knew they were with me.
... In any event, formal axiology—value science—appeared
to have come to stay. (Hartman, p. 38).*

*So, you are invited to read this chapter as a prelude to
Hartman's articulation of his theory of formal axiology. This
chapter also emphasizes the vital role that Hartman's interest
in matters of war and peace played in leading him to the
development of the value theory for which he is best known.*

*This essay has been edited for coherence by omitting one section
of approximately 1,000 words that were in the original. The
omission is marked by "☆☆☆".*

Suppose there was a man in your city who had the plague. You would
be disturbed, mobilize the department of health, isolate the person, and
watch carefully for other signs of disease in the population. Yet, plague
is only a way of dying—and leading to a death hardly more terrible
than that of being grilled in a moldering tank, being suffocated in a
sunken submarine, carbonized by a flamethrower, or seared by an atomic
explosion. But the germ that leads to these kinds of death is still free
and unchecked. The germ of war is still being breathed in and out in

our everyday talk and behavior. We do not fear this kind of death—in spite of the fact that in our lifetime it has killed more men, women and children than any other disease. War still is an accepted state of things with us; it is not yet regarded an abnormality, such as is a disease. We have not yet isolated the bacillus of war. This being the case, we justify our ignorance by rationalization, just as the people of the Middle Ages used to rationalize about the inevitability of epidemics. Today we know better concerning physical disease. Intrepid pioneers have conquered the forbidding territory of disease, built up the science of health and pro-phylaxis, of isolation and immunization. In the same way pioneers of peace must today do research into the social disease of war and lay the foundations for the health of the body politic—peace.

Comparing war with other diseases we are struck immediately by a significant difference. Diseases are attacks on our body by either organic or inorganic influences—microbes, bacteria, pollen, radiation, etc. War also is an attack on our body by either organic or inorganic influences—but war is more vicious than any other disease, for these influences are directed by human beings. Disease is evil on the subhuman level; war is evil on the human level. Research into the causes of war is research not into material or organic nature but into human nature. "Wars," we read in the constitution of UNESSCO, "begin in the minds of men, and it is in the minds of men that the defenses of peace must be construct-ed." The basis of peace in our time is a program of research and action concerning human behavior. Man, who has through medical science achieved fitness to live in his physical and organic environment must through peace research achieve fitness to live in his social environment.

***

Research into the minds of men is therefore as urgent a task for the nations as research into the properties of matter.

DEFINITION OF PEACE RESEARCH

Research into the minds of men would enable us to construct the defenses of peace. Research for peace would be research for normality. The reason such research has never been proposed is that we do not know what normality is. Much less do we know how to go about research in it. Yet, precisely such research is required if we want to learn the conditions of peace rather than those of war. When a mind is seized by mental illness the defenses of peace have already been destroyed. Research into mental illness is research into abnormality: it is already research into the conditions of war. Research into the conditions of peace is research into normal minds. Only if we know normality can we detect the beginnings of abnormality, the subtle deviations from normality which spell both insanity and its colossal counterpart, war. We are little interested, as yet in research concerning mental illness.[1] Much less are we interested in research concerning the imperceptible deviations from normality in which mental illness is rooted. For want of a better name, we shall call these deviations moral illness. Still less are we interested in research into moral health, or normality itself. The good, we seem to feel, takes care of itself. Actually, the good is our achievement. The evil takes care of itself.

Moral illness is beyond the point at which normality ends, just within the realm of abnormality, in the tensions of everyday life, our quarrels and disagreements, maladjustments and frustrations, prejudices and delusions. It is with moral illness that wars begin. In the words of a recent writer, "we have the roots of war in the home, the church, the school, in every family disagreement, in every church row, in every educational strife." We have it in every disappointment, every frustration, every maladjustment, every dislike, every jealousy, even in bad humor and bad luck. All these symptoms of strife, in all people, can grow together like the boils of a plague, to form one ghastly eruption. The ethical teachers of mankind have always seen war in this comprehensive light, as the sum total of all abnormal life situations.

On the other side of the line is the realm of normality, the world of appreciation and cooperation, enjoyment and satisfaction, open mindedness and imagination, in a word, the world of peace. It is a world of morality and values—of enhanced normality. Its roots, too, are found in all situations of life, in home and church and school and business. Peace research must investigate conditions of normality and abnormality in situations—from fitness for the particular task to fitness for the universe, from maladjustment in a job to cosmic maladjustment. The dunce and the devil, the monster and the saint, the hero and the coward, the bluff and the expert, all these and their situations must be examined by peace research. The whole scale of enhancement in normality, and debasement in abnormality, falls within the realm of this research. The new science of peace is a comprehensive discipline encompassing all life situations. It gives to these situations their essential meaning, whereas the other sciences give them restricted particular meanings. Peace is the sum total of all normal life situations.

RESEARCH INTO NORMALITY

In order to find the point at which normality passes into abnormality we must discover the minimum conditions of both normality and abnormality. To this end we cannot study abnormal phenomena, for here normality has already crossed the border line. We must study normal phenomena and follow their transition. But research into normality is more difficult than research into abnormality. The researcher into abnormality has definite phenomena to deal with; from definite points of attack he can survey the surrounding field. The researcher into normality has no such points to go by, his objective is the whole field; when he finds significant phenomena, it will be the lucky strike of a prospector. Yet it is precisely such prospecting research with which we must survey the field of normality. Only thus can we find out at which points normality becomes abnormality, social and moral health passes into social and moral illness, and peace assumes the symptoms of war.

We know that a nation is socially and morally ill when more and more children become criminal, families break up by the millions, divorce follows a third of all marriages, millions of drunks frequent the bars of the country each pay day. But do we recognize that a nation is sick when its people are torn apart by prejudice, its babies shocked by the millions in movie theatres, when the intellectual nourishment of millions of housewives is soap operas and that of their husbands the serials? Do we know that a nation is sick when its children are packed in stuffy schoolrooms and their teachers paid less than are streetsweepers? Are these symptoms of normality or abnormality? Do they spell peace—or war? Is it normality or abnormality when 31% of the people polled about the Bill of Rights have never heard of it; or when a stenographer in Chattanooga, asked about Dumbarton Oaks, answers she doesn't know, she only eats Shredded Wheat? Does it spell peace—or war, when 50 million people, 45 percent of all citizens, have a mental age of 12 or less; 9 million a mental age of nine and a half or less? Is our neglect of these things normal or abnormal?

When plants are retarded in growth, we know how to cure them; agricultural research stations dot the land, federal funds are appropriated by the millions for research relating to soil and erosion, the growth of≈trees and orchards. But there is no ethical research station, doing investigation into the soil of morality, the growth of man and his body and mind.

Without such research all other research is futile. Even the research into the weapons of war would be in vain, for it is research into the conduct of a disease rather than its cure and prevention. Peace research ought to be research into the minds of men. The question of this research ought to be not: how does nature work? But: how good is man? The majority of all existing research is directed toward the abnormal. What we need is research into normalcy—ethical research. Such research alone can lead us to intelligent action; for our greatest affliction at the present time is not so much ill will as ignorance of the good.

MORAL SCHIZOPHRENIA

The knowledge we lack is not technical knowledge. We are technical wizards. But, as it has been expressed, "we have discovered the right things in the wrong order. We have learned to control nature before we have learned to control ourselves." In doing so we have lost control even of our own inventions, and have thus magnified our chaotic emotions to global, if not cosmic proportions: we have made our world a monstrosity, mixing the noiseless efficiency of techniques with the groans of the tortured. We are scientific masters but moral morons. We suffer of moral schizophrenia, living in two worlds and two ages.

With our emotions we are still in the Stone Age, with our intellect we are projecting planetary travel. Our political institutions are rooted in the eighteenth century, some of our most "modern" societies use devices of classical tyranny—yet, we build the atomic plants of the next century. Man, in the words of a philosopher, is a rope stretched between the beast and superman. Technologically we are supermen, morally we are close to beasts. One more stretch, and the rope will snap; the superman will revert into beasts. To one society this reversal has already happened. The result was a nation of technological cannibals. What has happened to the Germans can happen to any nation. It is likely to happen if technological societies do not master their moral energies.

Modern man lives, as man always has, in danger of reverting to savagery. But the savagery of civilized man with his techniques and instruments is of a new and terrifying kind—it is the savagery of Drs. Jekyll and Moreau, and of their life counterparts, Drs. Schilling and Schumann, Wirth and Weber, Thiele and Mengele of Dachau and Auschwitz infamy. These men acted—not with disregard for, but studious attention to--human pain, driven by sadistic curiosity to know the workings of nature; they were not deaf to--but avidly interested in—the cries of tortured creatures. When civilized man loses his moral discipline, he becomes a monster, a savage not of the jungle but of technological precision, petty to "the strange colorless delight of intellectual desires," when "the thing before you is no longer... a fellow-creature, but a problem." Such, in the words of H.G. Wells, is the last culmination of scientific detachment. Men at the frontiers of science will be watched from now on with horrified suspicion. "Scientists of destruction" destroyed the cities of Warsaw and Hiroshima; tomorrow such scientists could destroy the globe. Scientists today are themselves terrified at the Frankenstein they have released. We have only experienced the dress rehearsal of the scientific monster. It is an outgrowth of our own desires, magnified by our intellect; it can be tamed only when we tame ourselves. We must now concentrate on our moral nature as thoroughly as we have devoted ourselves to the atom. The knowledge we lack is moral knowledge. We are as ignorant morally as we are expert scientifically.

The tension between moral ignorance and scientific knowledge cannot be relieved by scrapping knowledge. The only alternative is to apply the methods of scientific research to the nature of man. Our educated intellects must be joined by educated emotions to form moral intelligence. As it is, our moral and social life lacks all intelligent organization. Since we also lack the social instinct animals possess, it can be demonstrated that we live on a social level lower than animals.

We know how to handle machines efficiently because we make them efficiently. We also make ourselves, but we don't know this yet. Much less do we know how to make ourselves efficiently. Our character is supposed to grow almost by itself; educational systems are designed for the development of our intellect rather than that of our character. Actually, the production of a normal mature character is our greatest achievement.

Normality in technology means the use of every material to the end for which it is best fitted. Science and technology analyze every material and find methods for its optimum use. In the use of the most precious material, the human, we have not yet reached the intelligent, let alone the scientific stage. Thus, we fumble at every step, and instead of fitting each individual into the place where he can best develop his potentialities, professions and jobs are distributed helter-skelter with sad results both for individuals and for society. This is particularly noticeable when the leading jobs are given to unfit individuals.

In this respect we are lower than animals. Animals follow the one who is best fitted for the task of leadership. We do not choose our leaders at all with respect to their tasks, but according to chance, without any adequate, much less scientific system of selection. In the questions of social leadership, we live not only in two ages, we live on two different levels of evolution. Neurotics and knaves can become –and are becoming—leaders of complex technological societies.

As it is in society as a whole, so it is in particular life situations. The wrong man in the wrong place seems to be a more "normal" phenomenon than the right man in the right place. The majority of social maladjustments could be avoided if there existed a scientific system assisting everyone in his own development, in the knowledge of his own potentialities, and in finding his place in society. This task of human and social engineering, of fitting the right man for the right job, is a classical task of ethics. How little it has been begun, let alone fulfilled, is seen in the chaotic state of society. What is needed is a "Manhattan Project" of peace research.

THE EVIL OF IGNORANCE

The evil of our time, as that of all times, is due not so much to the evil in our hearts as it is to the ignorance of our minds. When a little old peasant woman zealously added another piece of wood to Johan Hus' stake a voice was heard out of the flames: "O sancta simplicitas!" When Pastor Schneider was hung up at Dachau, a skeleton with a crown of thorns on his head, SS-men around him spitting and whipping, he was heard to pray: "God forgive them for they don't know what they do." Massive evil is done out of ignorance rather than ill will. "The human pack," writes Goethe, "fears nothing so much as intelligence. Stupidity they should fear if they knew what is terrible."

Due to the massive evil of moral ignorance the best efforts of well-meaning men bog down in frustration and impotence. The Paris Peace Conference struck one European author as "the babble of spiritual midgets discussing the affairs of Lilliput." Due to the vagueness of social and moral ideas, diplomats, whose fingers could push the button for World War III, must feel their way to peace as through a fog. Diplomacy has become dilettantism. As a high official of the United Nations said to the head of the Rockefeller Foundation: "The chief thing we lack at the present time is knowledge—tested knowledge. We seem to have to guess our way along."

The science of peace is still in the mythical stage. One opinion seems as good as another and everyone believes himself to be an expert. What we need is a science of peace as precise as the sciences of physics and chemistry. Just as these sciences have developed from the vagueness of commonplace conjecture to precise disciplines, so the science of peace must develop from commonplace conjecture to scientific precision. The obvious categories of ethical behavior, such as good and evil, right and wrong, virtue and vice, self, value, freedom, choice, person, must be analyzed. They will probably lose in the process the fundamental importance present day ethics ascribes to them—just as the obvious categories of nature, sound, color, shape, and the like, have lost their fundamental importance in the natural sciences. In these sciences patterns and configurations of waves and vibrations, electrons and protons have, as primary qualities, replaced the sensuous secondary qualities of things. Similarly, we shall have to penetrate to the primary qualities of moral reality.

The natural sciences have developed methods which have brought gigantic natural powers within the reach of any individual able to turn a switch or push a button. Similarly, ethics will have to develop methods which will bring the moral powers of man within the reach of every individual. There will never be a moral push button, but there may be moral expertness.

A hundred years ago we were ignorant of the nature of electricity. The research of men such as Faraday, Maxwell, and Hertz clarified the exact nature of that power. The genius of practical inventors like Marconi and Edison brought it within the reach of every man.

Today we are ignorant of moral power. Theoretical research workers must define and analyze the power of man as it appears in the intricacies of human behavior. The genius of practical researchers must apply this knowledge to the management of individual and social affairs. The theoretical research into human nature must proceed as objectively and competently as does research into physical nature, and along lines dictated by logical necessity rather than practical consequence. "Just as the great advances of modern physical science have been made by men whose passion for understanding the facts of nature was greater than any concern with the practical social effects likely to follow from their inquiries, so the great advances of the future in ethical understanding are likely to be achieved only by those who are firmly resolved to press ethical inquiry to its logical limits without regard to immediate practical consequences." Theoretical research, thus defined by Morris R. Cohen, is to fashion the tools with which practical research can help organize social and personal behavior.

Due to our present ignorance of primary ethical categories, the divisions of methodology and ethical theory will have to be, for some time to come, the heart of the science of peace. The practical sciences are to apply whatever ethics methods are discovered, to their particular fields, and, on the other hand, to discover particular methods of their own with which to contribute to ethical method in general. If ethics is the science of social and moral normality, then the ethical methods, as a method of normalcy, ought to apply to every aspect of human existence and human endeavor. It ought to be capable of measuring the state of social and moral health in every particular situation—just as the thermometer, as common denominator for all deviations from the norm, measures the state of physical health.

Let us see whether such a method is possible.

THE METHOD OF PEACE AS A SCIENTIFIC METHOD

When the men of the Church looked through Galileo's telescope and saw the moons of Jupiter they pronounced them optical illusions; according to their knowledge no such moons could exist. Thus today many will pronounce a science of peace impossible. If it is, we must persist in our moral ignorance and let our machines exterminate life on earth. If we want to live we must conquer nature within us just as Galileo and his successors have conquered nature around us. Galileo had faith in the ultimate precision and rationality of nature. The first step of our own conquest may well be faith in the ultimate precision and rationality of our own nature. On Galileo's faith and his scientific method was built the structure of modern science; the inventors of our time stand, ultimately, on the shoulders of the men of the Renaissance. There is no reason why the conquest of human nature should not, in outline, be analogous to the conquest of physical nature. What we need today are both the Galileos and the Charles F. Ketterings of ethics.

The scientific method is a method of precision and abstraction. By abstraction is meant the isolation of particular aspects of phenomena for analysis, or the application of particular frames of reference to situations. By precision is meant the description of the isolated material with verbal concreteness and, eventually, mathematical exactness.

The Method of Abstraction

The disadvantage of abstraction is the fictitiousness of the phenomena described. In nature nothing is isolated. The isolated phenomena were "ideal cases" in which ideal laws were found. These laws were admirably exact and the methods of applying them to practical reality admirably ingenious. Yet the method of abstraction developed an obstacle to all true insight into nature, and into the nature of man in particular. It led to specialization among scientists which split up the community of scientists into tight departments. Even worse, it rent asunder our picture of nature into a mosaic of abstract features behind which the reality of nature disappeared. Nature as a whole does not appear in the field of vision of the specialized scientist; professionally he sees her only in the circumscribed field of his specialty. The scientific view of nature has often been accepted as the "true" view, with the result that philosophical and religious faith in reality was regarded as fiction. Actually, fiction was precisely the abstract robot called "nature." Particularly disastrous was this attitude for the knowledge of man himself. Man, as nature, was not seen as a whole. Rather was man considered in the abstract, a mosaic of ideal cases which, to a philosopher, make a textbook in pathology or psychiatry even today a nightmare of abstraction. Where is Man behind the special cases? Is he the exemplification of an ideal case or is he a human being in physical agony and mental anxiety?

The good physician must see man as a whole. He has his science only to guide him in the particular disease. But man is more than "the case," and to guide him in the knowledge of his patient—the sufferer—the physician has only his intuition. Similarly, he who wants to understand man as a whole has no science to guide him but only intuition—the same kind of intuition which must lead diplomats onward in their search for peace. While such intuition will always be indispensable ultimately, there is a large field in which it ought to be substituted by exact science.

All applied science requires two things: knowledge of ideal cases, or theoretical knowledge, and knowledge of the particular situation, or practical knowledge. For the former we have science, for the latter we have nothing. That there is no science of situations is due not so much to the insufficiency of the scientific method as to the inadequate application of that method to situations-as-whole. Whenever concrete situational problems are to be solved, the special sciences have to be integrated to form teams. The sciences cut life and nature apart into vertical strips, but situations are horizontal cross-sections of nature and life. To understand them the vertical strips must be sheaved together to form new units. In all concrete applications the method of abstraction must be complemented by a method of integration. There are no rules as yet for such a method, although during the war it was used with great success. But science has not yet caught up with the practice and therefore the practice cannot yet be universalized. Situationally integrated research during the war was called "operational research." It is this kind of research we must develop and apply to form the science of peace. The situation to which we must apply it is the behavior of man.

Obviously, we cannot treat all behavior at once. We must therefore abstract aspects of it. The scientific method of abstraction can be applied to human behavior if we find the clue to abstracting aspects of behavior without abstracting man. Every abstraction of ethical science must contain man-as-a-whole, even though in a specific configuration of situational circumstances. At present there is no science of man, just as there is none of situations, for the same reasons. Man has been cut up into dozens of different frames of reference, but no frame of reference has yet been applied to man-as-a-whole. The natural sciences were successful because they fitted appropriate frames of reference to natural phenomena. The framework of chemistry fits a chemical substance completely. Applied to man, that same framework will fit only very insufficiently—like a flea's coat measured to an elephant. Man transcends by far the chemical realm. What we have to find is a frame of reference adequate to the behavior of man-as-a-whole.

This frame of reference may be, precisely, his "situation," and it may be found by abstracting behavior itself.

Human behavior, like physical, chemical or any other "behavior," is process. It is a more complicated process than any other known, but the method of abstraction must be applicable to the social and moral as to any process: it must be capable of being analyzed into differentials, and these differentials capable of minute examination. The task of abstraction in the case of human behavior would thus be to isolate the process within which a particular behavior takes place, and then to view the particular behavioral situation as a differential of the process in question. The process must contain all the tendencies of the whole man. The differential of the process, the concrete situation under observation, must in turn contain all these tendencies, even though only differentials thereof. That is to say, each situational differential of process contains the differentials of all the features of the process. Ethical abstraction would thus find the whole man both in the analysis of the integral behavior process and in the synthesis of the situational differentials. We may call this the method of integral analysis and differential synthesis. Through investigation of the situational differentials, the situation appears as if under a microscope. It must, in the differential deviations from the integral behavior process, show up in the imperceptible deviations from normalcy with which we are concerned. Thus, the normality or abnormality of a particular situation ought to be determined. Such situational normality (or abnormality) may be called differential or microscopic normality (or abnormality). On the other hand, if the behavior process itself is abnormal, such abnormality ought to appear in the integral analysis of the process as a whole, as compared with other life processes. Such normality or abnormality may be called integral or macroscopic. In the case of abnormal process "normality" of the situation relative to the process would indicate absolute abnormality of the situation with respect to other life situations. Differential normality would be what we have called "relative" normality, integral normality what we have called "absolute" normality, or Peace.

Let us now investigate whether and in what way such normality or abnormality could be measured.

The Method of Precision

In order to measure a phenomenon, we need dimensions and standards by which to measure it.

Human and social process has more comprehensive dimensions than physical process. It contains the dimensions of physical process, space and time, but in addition the dimensions of personality and value, which in turn will have to be analyzed into their own dimensions. Personality alone may have at least four dimensions: the atomic, the chemical, the psychological, the conscious—each again with many subdivisions. The conscious may have its own four dimensions: consciousness, subconsciousness, imagination, and anticipation. The dimensions of the situation ought to be defined so as to determine the situation's "normalcy," that is to say its integration in and creative potentiality of the behavioral process in question. In as much as the different dimensions of the situation contribute to that integral potentiality, the situation is normal. If the process itself is normal, it is also moral.

We could measure the normalcy of the situation if all its dimensions were capable of measurement. The measurable dimensions of a situation are, at first sight, only space and time. Personality and value are, for the time being, not measurable, even though limited systems of measurement have been proposed by various scholars. It may be, however, that, as our insight into human situations grows, more and more facets of these situations will become accessible to measurement, until finally whole situations may be comprehended mathematically. The development of the physical sciences suggests such a possibility; one comprehensive system of formulae expresses practically the entire nature of the space-time field.

Situations, too, may be regarded as "field," as is already done by a substantial school of philosophers, psychologists and sociologists. For the present, knowledge of situational fields is crude. The development of the mathematical knowledge of physical energy fields took almost a century, from the lines of force of Faraday through the mathematical interpretations of Maxwell to the all-inclusive calculus of Einstein. In situational analysis we have not even reached the stage of Faraday, of seeing clearly the situational field pattern, let alone that of Maxwell or Einstein. But in all the sciences, sheaved together in situational analysis, patterns are emerging.

Consciousness can be investigated with the help of Gestalt psychology, which in time may evolve a pattern of the situational Gestalt. Atomic, chemical and physiological patterns are evolving in many different ways; the time is foreseeable, even though in a far-off future, when a personality will be exactly described by synthetic interpretation of its pattern genetic and cell structures, metabolic and hormonal patterns, the patterns of breathing, brain waves, of heart beats and tremors, of galvanic skin responses and blood pressure changes and, in addition, of the patterns of hand and face, fingerprints and handwriting, walking and eating. All these patterns are known but almost completely unexplored, much less coordinated. Here is a vast realm for ethical research, which may be classified under the name of morphology. A morphological study of values does not yet exist; studies in value measurements do, but these efforts are not integrated either. They form a task for value theory.

All in all it may be said that ethical measurement of situational dimensions at the present time ranges from exact numerical measurement as in the dimensions of space and time, through morphological Gestalt comparisons to completely uncharted realms. For the time being the Gestalt aspect of the various situational dimensions ought to be investigated—a gigantic task in itself. Later the various dimensional patterns may become integrated into a situational Gestalt. That such a situational Gestalt exists is proven by our synthetic view of situations. It is not impossible that, as a short cut, a relatively simple model of the situational Gestalt could be developed, which could lead on to further research, as did Bohr's model, to the research of atomic theory. Such a model ought to show the particular situation as a differential of behavioral process in general and ought to constitute a theoretical foundation of the empirical behavior curves found by psychologists. [2]

Situational Analysis

The first task of ethical research would then be to isolate behavior processes in integral analysis and to determine their differentials in differential synthesis. The next step would be either to state the dimensions applicable to these differentials and integrate them eventually into a situational pattern or, inversely, to differentiate a proposed pattern into the situational dimensions. The last step would be the analysis of the situational pattern by mathematical means. The whole program could be called one of Situational Analysis—operational research into situations.

Whereas this program is a very comprehensive one, unlikely to be completed in the course of one or even two generations, the future course can already be foreseen. It can also be understood that such a method would fulfill, eventually, the program of analyzing each situation with precision and measuring with exactness its deviation from the norm. Such a measurement would represent the moral measurement of the situation.

A good man, according to many teachers of ethics, is one who develops all his potentialities to the full. If man were seen as process, he would be good if every differential of the process, that is to say each situation, would in turn actualize to the full its own potentialities. The good in every situation would then be that tendency in it by which the situation contributes to the integral process of which it is part. A situation would be moral insofar as it is the normal differential of a normal process, or insofar as it contains potentially the integral process. The moral quality of a situation would be its potentiality or the creative quality by which a situation transcends itself and becomes part of the process. The moral logic of a situation—as against its scientific logic—would then be a logic of creativity. The good of the process itself would be both its integral and differential self-realization.

The isolation of moral situations by differential synthesis may not be easy; and even more difficult, at the present time, may be the precise determination of the moral quality in it. Yet, even now, when the method of precision is still in its infancy, not to say its prenatal state, certain procedures to determine that quality may be elaborated.

Differentials of process, or situations, may be the raw material of ethics as the science of peace, just as sounds, colors, and material things are the raw materials of the natural sciences. For the time being we may have to find the moral in situations as the chemist used to find radium in pitchblende—and it may be equally elusive. Situations are found in every field of human activity, and they may have to be precipitated from every such field. This "precipitation of situations" would have to be the task of the different social and "humanic" disciplines, which would supply ethics with its raw material—so to speak its pitchblends. The elaboration of the method of situational analysis, of discovering and measuring the moral in these situations would be the task of ethics itself.

Moral Skill

For the time being the method of precision will have to confine itself to linguistic definitions—a method in which ethical philosophers like Confucius and Socrates have seen one of the main tasks of ethics. Precise definitions of ethical terms ought eventually to end the confusion now prevalent not only in ethics but in all fields where ethical terms are used, like politics, economics, social science, public opinion, and the thoughts of the common man.

Although precision of verbal definitions is all-important in the present stage of ethical inquiry, its accomplishment is much more difficult than the analogous accomplishment in the natural sciences. These sciences deal with situations which, once isolated, present a comparatively simple picture. The situations of moral life are more complex. More perplexing, however, is another difficulty. In spite of the intricacy of human situations everyone today believes himself to be a social scientist, an economic expert, or a psychologist. It is the crux of most social and personal problems, and of the moral problem in particular, that they are not yet recognized as scientific problems to be tackled by experts only. Every person in the course of his life must solve such problems by the dozens. It has not yet dawned on humanity that the conduct of life is both an art and a science. In this case, truly, familiarity has bred contempt, and contempt for the art of living has led, ultimately, to skill in killing.

We all have to handle the raw materials of ethics every day, but we don't have to handle those of science. We have to crack the problems of our lives, but we don't have to split atoms. That is why we leave the latter task to the expert—and neglect meanwhile to make ourselves experts in the conduct of life. We can use material things without being scientists in the field—we can eat sugar without being chemists and use the radio without being engineers. But in the social disciplines we must be experts. At the present time we are dilettantes; we use politics without being statesmen, psychology without being intelligent, logic without being rational, and ethics without being moral. The results of our dilettantism are correspondingly inadequate; indeed, they are deadly.

All the disciplines of knowledge ought to be directed toward morality, that is toward peace. They ought to be applied to definite human situations as exactly and efficiently as electric power is used in lighting a room. The method of peace requires not only abstraction and precision but above all cooperation—the cooperation of all disciplines toward one aim: that of directing all knowledge toward the common denominator of man. The science of peace cannot be the work of one person, or of one school of men, but must be the cooperative effort of many scholars and many schools of thought.

THE INTEGRATIVE SCIENCE OF MAN

Before a science of peace can emerge, it will be necessary for the scientists of peace[3] to evolve their method and the social scientists to find them useful. The task of cooperation will be more difficult to fulfil than a corresponding task in natural science. There the test is simply: will it work? If it does, scientists cannot help but agree. In the social and moral sciences tests cannot yet be applied; the agreement of the scientists of peace is precisely the test of the working method. This agreement cannot be brought about by experiment and observation, but only by the compelling logic of procedure. In the natural sciences theories are discarded and accepted as experiments confirm or disprove them. In the social, and the moral sciences in particular, theories, experiments, and observation, are insolubly intermingled; they all have their being in the minds of the scientists. When an atomic bomb explodes there is no place to reason why it did so. The mechanism worked. When a man like Hitler or a people like the Germans explode there is no end to the interpretations. This is not due to the fact that social and moral phenomena are inaccessible to tests—the German experiment is an outstanding test of the fact that good must be active and evil does not pay—but to the fact that we have not yet developed the method to analyze such tests in all their multidimensional complexity. What we need now is agreement concerning such a method—and there is no method of getting such agreement.

The method to be agreed upon must be so comprehensive and yet so definite as to fit all the social phenomena. Each worker must be allowed to do ethical research in his own field and along different lines, until such time as the majority of research lines converge toward a single method. This method will then be adopted, almost as a matter of course. That such a method will eventually be developed seems to be implied in the logic of the present situation. Everybody agrees that integrative research is the next step in scientific inquiry. Such integrative research can well develop an integrative method. It is a common phenomenon in the history of science and technology that the same methods and inventions have been made at the same time at different places and from different points of attack. The method to be evolved may be the method of integral analysis and differential synthesis, the integrative method of moral situations. It may also be some other method. For the time being the method proposed is a hypothesis.

Thus, if there is ever to be a science of peace it must be an integrative science. Man lives on all the levels of existence, on the atomic of physics, the molecular of chemistry, as well as the biological of medicine and the rational of logic. He reaches from the atoms to the stars; all sciences must cooperate to chart his course in the situations of life. Many ethicists today believe that morality is rooted in the genes; a modern physicist like Schrödinger sees the genes as orderly aggregates of atoms which counteract the second law of thermodynamics. Morality would accordingly be based in atomic configurations and a tendency counteracting the law of entropy. On the other hand, man's moral character is seen to be founded not on the order of atoms but on the laws of the universe; Kant's admiration for the starry sky above him was coupled with his wonder about the moral law within him. God may not be a necessary hypothesis for science; he is, as Kant has taught and Niemöller demonstrated, a necessary postulate of morality.

Thus the science of man must cut across all the lines of scientific and even of metaphysical division. Like the decimals of irrational numbers to fill the gap between integers, so hyphenated sciences must be used to fill the gaps between the sciences—not only biophysics and biochemistry, but also psychophysics, psychobiology, social psychology, medical economics, psychosomatic medicine, social ecology, mathematical geography, gen-ethics, bioethics, zoological ethics, physical ethics, ethical physiology and ethical etymology (two sciences projected by Nietzsche), ethical musicology (projected by Plato), cosmic ecology and even perhaps, as suggested by Schopenhauer, cosmic demography and, a suggestion by Barlow Shapley, cosmic psychiatry.

If the science of peace is to be the science of normality it will apply the kind of research we have called "prospecting research." If it is to be the science of moral situations it will apply "operational research" in integral analysis and differential synthesis. It will be one of the tasks of the scientists of peace through prospecting research to define problems and formulate operational research projects. Many phenomena at present not subject to any science will have to be included in the program of peace research. To mention only a few at random: the problem of moral testing and measurement, of situational analysis and cartography, of analysis of patterns, of morphological valuation, of the relation between morality and time and space, of the physiological and zoological bases of emotions; the notion of the observer in social and natural science, of the spatiality and tempo of thought; the ethical analysis of concepts like process, actuality, potentiality, quality, quantity, order, disorder, energy, inertia, health and disease; the situational definition of terms like good, evil, right, wrong, virtue, vice, self, person, freedom, choice; institutions, representation, civilization, evolution, revolution, power; the examination of moral and social implications of language and mathematics; the ethical investigation of literature and music and the analysis of their situations by differential synthesis; the analysis of the relations between morality on the one hand, intelligence, musicality, and humor on the other; between prejudice and insanity, communication and compassion, voice and character; between parental love and child morality and between hormones and parental love; the connection between technology and reproduction, between the trauma of birth and moral development; between subliminal stimuli and tact, and between tact and taste.

The result of the new science, or rather, the new direction of research, ought to be a new discipline with methods as accurate as the present methods of the social sciences, and eventually as exact as those of the natural sciences. The new science ought to be taught eventually in every school, as is physics today, and on every campus. Thus everybody, eventually, ought to be able to apply to every life situation moral standards: the selection of an employee or a political candidate, the choice of a profession or a mate, the buying of a car or of education, ought to proceed along ethical lines.

The science of peace would lay, thus, the theoretical foundations of a better world. It would enable educational and other organizations creative of good will to gauge and direct their work scientifically. By lifting moral phenomena from the emotional to the scientific plane, it would take the wind out of the sails of professional and other haters: we cannot hate what we know scientifically. It would add to the space-time world the moral dimension. Thus it would contribute to the reformation by which the world of technical science must become the world of moral conscience.

The Moral Reformation

The integration of the sciences over the common denominator of Man will bring about a new insight which must open the narrow divisions of custom to the vision of a moral universe. Today, through the cosmic theory of Einstein, and the atomic theory of Planck and others, science has put into the hands of man the power of the sun itself. Man, through science, now stands at the crossroads of cosmic morality. He can choose good, and thus guarantee the success of his terrestrial adventure, or evil, and thus conclude it "for good." The atomic bomb, in splitting the nucleus, has fused the physical and the moral universe. From now on both are one. From now on we must either live morally, that is normally and abundantly, or die. To die is easy; all we have to do is to persist in provincialism, greed, and inertia. To live morally is difficult; we must have vision, generosity, and genius. If we muster them, the promise of good is as infinite as the portent of evil is definite. There will be opened to us a new earth and a new heaven, "Man's capacities," says a philosopher, "have never been measured nor are we to judge what he can do by any precedent." His potentialities are unbounded; his faith can move mountains and his thought lift the earth in its angles. He has conquered the power of the stars. He has conquered space and time on his planet and will soon conquer the space between planets. On his globe he is virtually omnipresent; his voice can be heard, and soon his picture seen, at one and the same time all around the globe. His mind can communicate with every other mind on earth in a flash. His body can move around the earth in less time than it takes to walk through a large city. Man's body and mind span the earth. Once he has conquered his soul he will span the universe.

Between the good of tomorrow and the evil of today stands the ignorance of man about himself. If only a fraction of the effort used for preparation and conduct of war would be used for research into peace, the chances of man's survival would be immeasurably increased. What we need for this research are not instruments nor techniques nor experiments to speak of, but only Thoughts. The science of peace is to be an organization of thinkers directed toward one aim. In terms of money thoughts are not expensive; in terms of profit they are the most fruitful investment possible. The moral future is among us, but it cannot be reached with gadgets nor through the patent office; it must start from within. The proposed science will not perform conspicuous deeds; the good does not explode; it grows organically.

The moral reformation will be as inconspicuous as is everything normal. It will widen the scope of human action, but into realms which are not those of space and time and therefore not as awe-inspiring as the flight of a rocket. Yet, the reformation will be an experiment in creative civilization greater than any before. It will open new dimensions to common man and make the moral as natural to him as electricity is today. As the revolution of the Renaissance burst open the narrow circle of Aristotelian science and conquered material nature, so the reformation of today must burst open the pigeon-holes of specialization and conquer man's moral nature. The cooperative power which split the atom must be used to fuse into unity an atomic society. By a project similar to the Manhattan Project in scope but infinitely more rewarding and less expensive, we can live up to the challenge of this age. Natural science, by analyzing material qualities into quantities, not only made things accessible to mathematical measurements but created new things with qualities previously unheard of and powers undreamed of. Similarly the new ethical science of the future, by analyzing moral qualities, will not only make human nature accessible to conceptual thought, but will create for man powers hitherto undreamed of. By its reference to the moral dimensions it will show up war in all its bestiality, inhumanity, and inefficiency—a nightmare of abnormality, and peace as the creative well-defined enterprise of normality. The age of quantity and force is at an end, the age of quality and spiritual power must begin.

The Conquest of War

The conquest of war will be achieved by substituting the logic of quantity by the logic of quality. Once man's nature is known in quantitative measurements his potentialities will develop to new qualities. His present thought, welded like the animal's to the moment in space and time, will elevate itself first to comprehend the succession of moments in space and time, and then to leap into the infinity of the spiritual universe where men are brothers. The first task will be achieved by man's capacity of moral analysis, the second by the logic of his soul.

The Sense of Process

The sense of process is nothing but the capacity of situational moral analysis, possessed by intuitively moral individuals. Such intuitively moral individuals may be called geniuses of morality, in the same sense that Gauss may be called a genius of mathematics and Edison a genius of technology. A genius pioneers a field by intuition; the act of pioneering is precisely the achievement of making the field accessible to the average man's logic. Gauss and Edison often had the results—the 1% inspiration—but what they needed was the logical way to get there—the 99% perspiration. So there are geniuses of morality who possess the sense of process but who must make it accessible, by some logical method, to the everyday logic of the average man.

The sense of process has not yet been analyzed scientifically—this analysis, precisely, is the task of the Science of Peace—but it has been described by philosophers and poets. It is the capacity to transcend the momentary, to see the potentialities of the situation and to insert the situation into the dream of human and cosmic events.

For a description of the sense of process let us turn to Rebecca West and her interpreter, Clifton Fadiman in his Foreword to Tolstoy's *War and Peace*[4]. We can do no better than follow Fadiman in his exposition, not only because of its unusual ethical acumen, metaphysical insight, and historical vision, but also because of the tremendous importance of the matter of our subject. It gives a fitting summary, and illustration of our method of peace.

In Rebecca West's *Black Lamb and Grey Falcon* there is a long conversation between Miss West and her husband concerning the character of one of their companions—whom they do not like—in their travels through Yugoslavia. Gerda is a German woman married to a Serb. Though politically no Nazi, she is one spiritually. I should like to quote briefly from the long analysis Miss West's husband makes of the character of Gerda because I think it throws light on the character of Hitler and of the Nazi type generally, and re-enforces the analysis Tolstoy makes of the character of Napoleon.

"Gerda has no sense of process. That is what is the matter with Gerda. She wants the result without doing any of the work that goes to make it.... She is angry because we have some money. She feels that it might just as well belong to her... For her, the money might as easily have been attached to her as to us by a movement as simple as that which pastes a label on a trunk... as she has no sense of what goes to bring people love, or friendship, or distinction, or wealth, it seems to her that the whole world is enjoying undeserved benefits; and in a universe where all is arbitrary, it might just as well happen that the injustice was pushed a little further and that all these benefits were taken from other people, leaving them nothing, and transferred to her, giving her everything. Given the premise that the universe is purely arbitrary, that there is no causality at work anywhere, there is nothing absurd in that proposal. This is the conqueror's point of view... Let us admit it, for a little while the whole of our world may belong to Gerda. She will snatch it out of hands too well bred and compassionate and astonished to defend it. What we must remember is that she will not be able to keep it. For her contempt for the process makes her unable to conduct any process.... To go up in an aeroplane and drop bombs is a simple use of an elaborate process that has already been developed. But you cannot administer a country on this principle.... Gerda's empire... will be an object of fear and nothing else. For this reason, I believe that Gerda's empire cannot last long. But while it lasts it will be terrible. And what it leaves when it passes will also be terrible.

For we cannot hope for anything but a succession of struggle for leadership among men whose minds will have been unfitted for leadership by the existence of tyranny and the rupture of European tradition, until, slowly and painfully, the nations re-emerge, civilization re-emerges."

Now Tolstoy's depiction of Napoleon is the depiction of a man who has lost his "sense of process." Though he speaks of himself as a Man of Destiny, he does not believe in destiny, does not believe that human history is continuous. He believes, instead, that he can arrest its course or divert its direction because he wishes to do so.

Tolstoy himself, on the other hand, wrote *War and Peace* in part to express his sense of the thick continuity of human events, the multitudinous linkages which even a Napoleon cannot break. It is those characters who have an awareness of this continuity, like Prince Andrew, that he admires. It is those characters who have no such awareness that he scorns. The Tolstoyan viewpoint is evidenced even in the creation of such minor personages as the fatuous Berg who, simply because he is himself, is convinced that everything he does is right. A more significant example is the aristocratic waster, Anatole Kuragin, "who regarded his whole life as a continual round of amusement which someone for some reason had to provide for him." It is this inability to conceive reality which is to ruin the class Anatole represents. It is the lack of a sense of process on the part of an insulated class which is to lead straight to 1917 in Russia. Someday it may be shown that it led also to Pearl Harbor.

Now, from time to time, as Miss West reminds us, a group of powerful people deficient in a sense of process arises and for a time dominates the world or a part of it. They are able to affect such domination because this lack of a sense of process is a great strength. The Nazi is automatically insulated from the doubts, hesitations, and fears of those of us who possess such a sense. And, if the world were so simple that fanatical courage and superhuman energy could control it, Hitler, the man with no sense of process, would succeed permanently.

But, as Tolstoy reminds us, the world is not so simple. History is far more complicated than even the most wide-visioned conqueror (and Hitler's perspectives, one must admit, are enormous) can understand. In the end the Hitler-type is defeated by his inability to judge his own limitations.

Thus, the man without a sense of process identifies with the moment, in monumental contempt of the dynamics of the world.[5] Yet, that dynamic finally fails him. The man who lacks the sense of process has situational consciousness only, he lacks the temporal dimension, his consciousness is spatial, like the instinct of animals. His genius, to speak with Nietzsche, resides in his nostrils[6]. Thus he clings to the nearest like a dog on the trail, able to sense the scent of the things at hand, but unable to feel the curse of things to come. He cannot anticipate, because he cannot count with potentialities. Therefore there is always the moment of the great, seemingly unexplainable blunder, like Napoleon's and Hitler's attack of Russia, Hitler's failure to invade England after Dunkirk and the Japanese failure to invade California after Pearl Harbor. On the other hand, there are and will always be the seemingly miraculous salvation of the good people, like the battle of the Marne, the evacuation of Dunkirk, the battles of Stalingrad and El Alamein, or the miraculous "breaks," like the undamaged Rhine bridge at Remagen. These "breaks" are so in a double sense; breaks for the good and breaks for the evil. For the good it is the final breakthrough of long absent potentiality into reality, for the evil it is the break of the causal chain— the moment when the improvisation of the creative mind is needed and where the scheming mechanical mind of the man without sense of process fails. At that moment, when the long neglected dynamics makes itself felt again after the freakish interlude, the scales of history are balanced again. It is the moment when God, after having permitted the play of the unreal within the real for some time, gets bored with it, in Victor Hugo's tremendous phrase[7], and takes up the original impulse again. At that moment "time wreaks its majestic vengeance upon everything that is fragmentary," in Hegel's words, a majesty of time which it was our generation's privilege to witness in gigantic form. Then the false gods tumble into the dust, their glory becomes shabby and their palaces rubble. Then the little men, those for whom "time works," write their tourist signatures on the ruins of broken capitals. They have the sense of process and they break, determinedly yet casually, what the senseless had built "for a thousand years." They know, as a navy strategist said at Pearl Harbor, that one can plan up to a point, that one can have certain theories, but "after that there is the Jesus factor—the unpredictable always works for the good. Time is on the side of the good, for in time the good is, by definition, realized. Therefore also, to be good, you need time. One cannot be in a hurry. But if you have time the good will prevail. Lincoln expressed it in the words that you can fool all the people some of the time and some people all the time, but not all the people all the time. Plato expressed it in the words that the unjust are like runners good at the start only, "they go off at great pace, but in the end only look foolish, slinking away with their ears dragging on their shoulders and without a crown; but the true runner comes to the finish and receives the prize and the crown."[8]

The good man has the sense of process, the intuitive logic of potentialities that is part of the ethical. He can anticipate. Thus he does not have to fear the moment of vengeance and retribution; he is part of the dynamic process itself. Hence things "come along his way," they "work out." Thus Truth will always prevail—even though many times it may look ever so impossible. And it always will and must look so, as long as the sense of process is unconscious in a person. Only when it has become conscious and differentiated into a method, will the sense of doom leave humanity.

At that time confidence in human destiny will be as universal and natural as is today confidence in tomorrow's sunrise.

Such a confidence in human destiny will be an event of unheard of novelty. It will add a new dimension to the human race. It will be like a leap unto a higher species—a spiritual mutation. It will endow man with the logic of the spiritual—a logic transcending space and time. The logic of Jesus, now largely unknown and unobeyed, will become the logic of man.

THE LOGIC OF JESUS

The logic of Jesus is a spiritual logic, liberated from space and time. Scientific logic—the logic of Galileo and Newton, Einstein and Planck—had conquered the physical universe. It is now ready through the conquest of man's own nature to comprehend the spiritual universe. This universe was called by Jesus the Kingdom of God.

The Kingdom of God is not a kingdom of "idealistic" unreality. On the very contrary, it is the kingdom of reality—and therefore of success. The kingdom of the material world, although it has been conquered by man, has not brought success to man. It has brought him to the verge of extinction and has increased his sufferings millionfold. It has been a failure of man. The scientific logic, in order to be a success, must be implemented by a spiritual logic.

This logic is very simple. It is the logic of creativity of which we spoke, of seeing each situation in the stream of human and cosmic events. The logic of Jesus is the logic of creative situational potentiality.

Since the Kingdom of God is not of this—material—world it is of a world beyond space and time. It is not too difficult to imagine such a world. In a world without space and time there is no separation. There are no finite bodies or things. There is only unity of mind and spirit. In so far as we, with our minds and spirits, are members of the spiritual world, we are one with every other member, for there is no separation between us and others. Neither is there displacement from one place to another. In the spiritual world nothing can be taken away. What one has all have and what one has not, none have. Since nothing can be taken away every event in that world profits all. It is a world of accretion and increment. In that world the logic of mathematics does not count. The logic of Jesus knows no subtraction but only addition. The part and the whole are one and the same. In the Kingdom of God the first is the last and the last is the first, for they are all partners in the same realm. It makes no difference in that kingdom whether a man has worked a day or whether he has worked a minute; both will get the same penny, as do the workers in the vineyard, for it makes no difference who has what, since what one has all have. The only crime in the kingdom of heaven is to be barren, as the fig tree, or to be selfish with one's potentialities, as the man who buried his talent; "for unto everyone that hath shall be given, and he shall have abundance; but from him that hath not shall be taken away even that which he hath." The greatest joy in the kingdom of heaven is the return of the lost, for nothing can be lost in that kingdom unless it be uncreative. The prodigal son and the lost sheep are still treasures in the kingdom of heaven and seeds of potential growth.

This logic is utterly different from our space-time logic of quantitative addition and subtraction, which lies at the basis of all our thinking, whether in the retribution of "justice," the greed for material profit, or the lust of "power." We must learn the logic of Jesus if we want to succeed. It is the logic of the mother who loves the second child as much as the first, without for that matter diminishing the love to the first. It is the logic of the teacher who gains the more he gives of his knowledge to his pupils, and whose greatest sorrow would be not to have men equaling him in understanding and inspiration. It is the logic of Lincoln who annihilated his enemies by making friends out of them. It is the logic of the African tribe that condemns a murderer to marry the widow of the murdered man in order to produce a life for the one he has taken. It is a logic which presupposes the creative cooperation of one's fellow men in his own selfish aims. Such creative transformation of unselfishness begets brotherhood. It is this logic which performs miracles; it is the logic of the feeding of the four thousand with seven loaves of bread.[9]

These miracles came about by enlisting the greatest resource of the world, namely man, in a common enterprise. The technique of such miracles is simply the logic of creativity as expressed in the teachings of Jesus. It is this logic which we must scientifically discover and practically use. Only thus can we overcome the mechanistic, quantitative logic of our private and public life. It is an easy logic if we will do just one thing: set the human person into the center of every situation.

For in man alone resides potentiality. In his unlimited potentiality resides his very humanity.[10] Therefore Jesus was the one person on earth who "so far as the records go, has shown a respect for personality utterly and without reservation. Christ consorted with harlots and sinners neither in condescension nor without recognition of their sins: he thought of them quite naturally, quite as a matter of course one might say, as fellow human beings, and therefore to him as a man, essentially and beyond their sins, his equals.[11] For Jesus every human being was a symbol of, and a candidate for, the Kingdom of Heaven. Each human individual for Him was a partner in the enterprise of human-divine cooperation. All we have to do is to rediscover in every human being the supreme value.

This is man's potentiality of becoming. In every man we must see, foster, and educate the possibility of growth. We must abolish all forms of compulsion which obstruct the physical, mental, or spiritual growth of men, whether it be the crippling effect of material poverty, the strait-jacket of totalitarian dogma, or the insanity of prejudice. We must abolish these obstacles to growth by the creative method of enlisting the help of their victims, the poor, the dogmatic, the prejudiced. We must appeal to the human aspiration in all man. We can never overcome these things by force—whether it be the laws of Congress, loans of dollars, or loads of bombs. Only the inspiration of men creatively guided by a working method can overcome the deadlock of power and bring about peace.

[1] In the fiscal year 1946-1947 the federal government spent $11,500,000,000 for the armed forces--$7,300,000,000 for the Army and $4,200,000,000 for the Navy. Of this the Navy spent $70,000,000 for "basic research," the Army Air Forces $185,000,000, and the ground forces $100,000,000-a total bill for research of $730,000,000. The Manhattan Project cost an additional $375,000,000—a total for war research and development in the last fiscal year of $730,000,000. The National Mental Health Act, proposing the expenditure of $7,500,000 for research into mental and nervous illness—a sum equivalent to one percent of the appropriation for war research and to one fifteenth of one percent of the total war budget—has not been acted upon either by the 79th or 80th Congress.

[2] Such a model of the situational Gestalt is the subject of a forthcoming book by the present author.

[3] We may call them "ethicists," since ethics is the science of situations, from Greek "…" or "…" [indecipherable], the root of Latin "situs."

[4] Simon and Schuster, New York, 1942, p. xlviii ff.

[5] This is the theme of Max Picard's book, Hitler Within Ourselves, Human Events Associates, Chicago, 1947. This book is a "must" read for everyone interested in the logic of peace. Also, Rauschning, The Revolution of Nihilism; Giano's Diaries of Mussolini; General Marshall's The Winning of the War in Europe and the Pacific.

[6] Ecce Homo, Why I am a Fatality.

[7] Concerning Napoleon after the Russian campaign, when disaster upon disaster dogged his footsteps: "God was bored by him."

[8] Republic, x 613.

[9] The technique of this "miracle" is beautifully described in Lloyd Douglas' The Robe.

[10] "We have given thee, Adam, no fixed seat, no form of thy very own, no gift peculiarly thine, that,--as the thirsty drink--, thou mayest feel as thine own, have as thine own, possess as thine own the seat, the form, the gifts which thou thyself shalt desire. A limited nature in other creatures is confined within the laws written down by Us. In conformity with thy free judgment, in whose hands I have placed thee, thou art confined by no bounds; and thou wilt fix the limits of thy nature of thyself. I have placed thee at the center of the world, that from there thou mayest more conveniently look around and see whatsoever is in the world. Neither heavenly nor earthly, neither mortal nor immortal have We made thee. Thou, like a judge appointed for being honorable, art the moulder and maker of thyself; thou mayest knead thyself into whatever shape thou dost prefer. Thou canst grow downward into the lower natures which are brutes. Thou canst again grow upward from thy mind's reason into the higher which are divine."

[11] Victor Gollanzc, Our Threatened Values.

CHAPTER V
Report from Europe

EDITOR'S NOTE

In the summer of 1946, only a year after the War ended, Hartman visited Europe on a trip sponsored—it seems—by an association of churches of which he was a part. Given its tone of voice, this essay reads as if it was a speech or a lecture given to members of his sponsoring organization upon his return.

Hartman also authored a second report from his trip, entitled, "The Treatment of Displaced Persons in Sweden." He reports there favorably and in more detail about Sweden's warm embrace and support of war refugees. That second report is not published here but is alluded to by Hartman in several places.

He writes here that this [1946] visit "was my second return to Europe since I left it on the day of Munich, in October 1938. By this day , he refers to what became known as the Munich Agreement, wherein the U.K., France, and Italy reached an agreement with Nazi Germany that Germany could annex the Sudetenland territory of Czechoslovakia. This act of appeasement was supposed to put an end to the expansionism of Germany, thus preventing the expansion of Hitler's war. It did not. It was the act that prompted Hartman, with his wife Rita and their infant son, Jan, to leave Sweden for the U.S., then Mexico.

What prompted Hartman to return to Europe in 1939, and how long he stayed, is not known to me. It is not mentioned in his Autobiography, nor in any papers that I have come across. Perhaps the 1939 visit was a business trip taken as part of his work for Walt Disney.

He writes in this essay that the 1939 trip left him with "a sudden choking in my throat. The atmosphere was tense, very much like what I had once encountered in an insane asylum on my flight from the Nazis." This is a reference to the occasion in 1933 when he decided to flee Germany, as he wrote about in his autobiography, Freedom to Live *and elaborated upon in even more detail in the as-yet-unpublished manuscript, "On God's Side."*

In this report, Hartman recounts many stories of personal hardship and tragedy endured by Europeans during the war. But its tone, on the whole, is an optimistic one.

The essence of Hartman's report is captured in one paragraph:

I learned also that the economic and political problems with which we are so much concerned are trivial as compared with the problems of the human soul with which we are so little concerned. War and peace, I now know, are not problems of politics or economics or geography or bureaucracy. Rather, they are problems of the human heart.

I want to give you a report from Europe, based on my experiences during this summer of 1946. I visited only three countries: Sweden, Denmark, and England, and flew over the ruins of Hamburg—a horrible sight. But I interviewed and talked with literally hundreds of people including members of my family who are in or who have travelled in Norway, Finland, Belgium, Holland, France, Italy, Switzerland, Austria, Germany, Poland, and Russia. In addition I visited Rehabilitation camps for so-called Displaced Persons (an inhuman enough name for an extremely moving assemblage of human beings). They told me of conditions in Rumania, Hungary, Czechoslovakia. Finally, I draw upon a large correspondence, coming mainly from Germany. In this way I have gained an overall impression of the situation on the continent, and it is this composite picture which I want to present to you today.

This was my second return to Europe since I left it on the day of Munich, in October 1938. Why had I left? Because on that day, eight years ago, I saw the continent doomed to disaster. Family and friends told us we were making the mistake of our lives in leaving Europe at that time, that there would never be a war. The reaction from friends in America was the same when we arrived here. But, approaching the European coast on my return in January 1939, I felt a sudden choking in my throat. The atmosphere was tense, very much like what I had once encountered in an insane asylum on my flight from the Nazis. Europe was mentally deranged; it was insane. Very few people then diagnosed the disease clearly or felt the incipient outbreak of it. Only gradually have I come to understand the real meaning of my almost instinctive aversion to the continent at that time. It was a reaction against disease, against the moral disease which the philosopher Friedrich Nietzsche had analyzed in a brilliant essay written the same year Adolf Hitler was born, that disease which was to break out just four months after I had left the continent for good.

This time, in June of 1946, the return was, I must say, a glorious one. Europe was still there, the Europe of cliffs and rocks, of blue sky, of gardens and lakes, of the small red houses of Sweden. Even the people of Europe were still there. Now the atmosphere was gay and cheerful. The tension was gone. With the acute stage of the disease over, the continent breathed like a person just feeling the powers of health after a serious illness. She is by no means healthy yet; the microbes are still in her blood, but they are fighting a losing battle. The devil has departed; the good has another chance. Thus, in a period when insensitive people—business-men, senators, journalists, even diplomats—babble about another war, you will hear from me not a message of despair, but one of hope, indeed of promise. Peace may be as improbable today as war was in 1938, but as surely as I was a prophet of gloom at that time, I am now a prophet of peace. And I speak not as a fool in a fool's paradise. I know the powers which Europe sapped from men of good will during the infamous years of Hitlerism, and I know now the powers that Europe is restoring to these same men. When I speak of the future of Europe I do so not as a bystander idly watching the course of history; rather do I speak as an actor in the great drama of the world. For the future of Europe is your future and mine. I come home from this journey with unlimited confidence in the power of the human spirit. War and peace are in our hands. If we despair, we despair of our own selves. But if that is the case, we have no right to live in these times when Europe has given to the world saints and martyrs, heroes of a new moral future. Let me speak of them first so that you may understand more deeply the terrifying disease which Europe has, in spite of everything, survived.

The mere fact of survival, the simple realization that Europe is still there, was my first strong impression. Not only the landscape is there, but the people too. Admittedly, a great part of the landscape has been changed; there are stretches without a tree or vegetation, without a single stone left standing. But by far the greater part of the land is still ready to bear fruit, slowly, it is true, but surely. From Dublin to Ankara, from Moscow to Lisbon, most of the cities, towns, and villages are still there, pulsing with life. Even the people remain. Those who have fallen number thirty million Europeans. More phantasmal after the avalanche is the fact that 350 million have survived, many of them by the skin of their teeth. If the dead are victims of hitherto unheard-of human depravity which deprived them of even the most primitive dignity of death, many of these living are examples of the incredible power of the human spirit. I have seen so many of these people that I scarcely know which to describe first. Sweden has admitted to her shores, often from the very doors of the gas chambers, 20,000 human wrecks. Together with another 60,000 refugees from all parts of Europe, she has admitted a number which in percentage of population would correspond to our having admitted, 1,600,000 Displaced Persons. Actually, we admitted 962, whom we confined behind barbed wire in the state of New York. Eventually after long debate in Congress, these people were turned loose to shift for themselves. Sweden is systematically rehabilitating these people and integrating them into her economic life. Through the courtesy of the Swedish Government, I was shown some of the camps and schools by one of the officers in charge of the whole program. Most of the people, especially those between the ages of 14 and 19, look as normal and ruddy as any of us. But the stories they have to tell are really hair-raising.

I have not time for all of it, or even for a small part. Shall I tell of the girl who showed me the dog bites on her arms? She was strapped to the earth by an SS-woman and dogs set upon her. Today she lives. That same girl showed me a more horrible scar on her leg. This was the result of a human bite. For twelve days she was packed with 120 skeleton-like human beings in a steel freight car designed for 48 persons or 8 horses, without food or water, her arms upstretched. Some of the unfortunate slumped down into the mass of legs; once down no one could help them. In their agony of suffocation they bit the legs of the people around them. "But the worst," this girl said, "was when we finally left the car. There was nothing left of those who had collapsed. We were wearing wooden shoes and had trampled them into a bloody mass." This girl is Eva Hochteil, from the town of Oradea in Rumania. She is a husky girl now, weighing 160 pounds. When she was brought to Sweden she weighted sixty pounds—sixty, and had typhus, dysentery, and tuberculosis. Now she is finishing high school and wants to go to college. What she needs is sixty dollars a month for one year. This is but one case.

I saw and spoke to hundreds of others; there are millions of them all over Europe. One girl from Lithuania whom I met had once been thrown away as a typhus corpse to be burned. As the Germans carried the corpses out it became dark and, as she explained it, "some of us corpses remained there." She then woke up and crawled away. When I saw her she was enthusiastically leading a group of sixty girls in song, keeping time by stomping with her feet. To my question about her survival she answered, "I wanted to live. But that I am alive is due to a higher power."

I met one couple who lived through this entire war in a hole in the earth, like moles, and who consequently lost their sight. Today they work in a textile factory. I met a boy who lived for four years in a chest of drawers, hidden away by merciful parents. His legs are crippled, but he lives.

I met a girl, Hanka Weintraub, from Cracow, a Jewess who was forced to dig a grave for her mother, shot down before her eyes. By some quirk of fate she obtained Aryan papers and worked as a secretary for the German ration board for the town of Lodz. At a party she sat beside Hans Frank, the governor of Poland and butcher of Polish Jews, who passed her the dishes most gallantly. After the party she was driving home with a Nazi when an old Jew crossed the street. The Nazi accelerated to run over the old man, Hanka screamed and pulled the wheel away from him. He looked at her in astonishment and said, "It's a Jew!" "Yes," she said, "but it is a man!" Never have I heard the word "man" spoken with so much emotion as by this girl when she told me the story. After three months she could not bear her role anymore and reported to a concentration camp for Jews. Today she is a chubby, pretty girl, a nurse in a TB home—she also had TB and a host of other diseases—and in a few years she will be a doctor. Hans Frank, the governor of Poland, will then be dead. Today he weeps daily in his cell at Nuremberg and prays to Saint Florian, the protector saint of Poland.

I could go on telling you the stories of men and women I met on this trip, in comparison with which all the drama of literature would be commonplace and even a character like Oedipus, who killed his father, married his mother, and blinded himself, would be an everyday person. I could tell you of the woman doctor who assigned her own child to be burned, of the mother who had to shove her husband and two children into the furnace of Haidanek, of the Rabbi who performed a funeral service over some cakes of soap, the material reminder of his congregation whom the Nazis had manufactured into soap. I could tell you about the work of the Swedish government in recreating these physical and mental spectres into human beings. They all live—how often have I heard the words, "We were dead and are reborn. We are now living our second life." They all live, some still in a stupor but many of them with a deeper consciousness of life than most of us will ever have. They live just one day's journey from here. They are not figments of the imagination even though they have lived through problems of the heart which no poet could ever conceive—simply because no poet ever dared to stray so far from reality. Only the insane imagination of the Nazis has made possible these impossible things, and therein, as Thomas Mann has suggested in his preface to the novels of Dostoevsky, the imagination of the people of poets and musicians has finally described its full demonic way.

For what you and I have been saying is merely so many words; I can appeal only to your imagination. For me this was a living experience. If you had been with me you would understand how deep was Europe's sickness, indeed how deep it is still. Yet, although you would have seen misery beyond your conception, you would in the very depth of understanding, have found new hope. For you would have seen proof that however colossal are the forces of destruction, the forces of life are greater. In these camps the whole abysmal depth of the European problem, indeed the world problem, lay open before my eyes. And not only before my eyes, but before those of everyone who had to do with these people, even before their own eyes. I learned that the problem of the world is a problem of the human heart, a moral problem. And I learned more about the nature of morality than any book or any professor ever taught me. I lived through, even though vicariously, the problems of ethics. I learned also that the economic and political problems with which we are so much concerned are trivial as compared with the problems of the human soul with which we are so little concerned. War and peace, I now know, are not problems of politics or economics, or geography or bureaucracy. Rather they are problems of the human heart. No businessman can fathom them, no senator, no journalist, no diplomat. The so-called peace conference in Paris is like the babble of spiritual midgets discussing the affairs of Lilliput.

What we need is a new set of leaders, moral leaders. The people of Europe who have been in touch with the Nazi sickness and who have in some way survived, do see the true problems now. In the countries which had to endure Nazi occupation there is a new vitality which I had not expected. This was my second strong impression on my return to Europe this summer. It is a vitality not only of the spirit but also of the mind, involving economic and political awareness. It is wrong to say that Europe is in Chaos, that she is starving. It is wrong to generalize about Europe at all. Certain regions are in chaos and in others there is starvation. But there are also regions which are in better order politically and which enjoy greater economic wealth than does the United States. These regions are Sweden and Switzerland. Let me give them a grade of A on an economic comparison. By this same standard, the United States would rate an A-. Ireland and Czechoslovakia B, Denmark, Norway, and Belgium B-, C+ would go to France and Finland, C to Holland and England, C- to Russia. Italy and Portugal I would give D+ with D for the other still feudal countries, for example Spain in the west and the Balkans in the east. The lowest designation is F for Germany and Austria.

This is a very rough estimate, but it does give at least some idea of the economic situation on the continent today. Let me add that the countries in the A to C category are countries of unlimited economic possibility. The field is open to any enterprising young man to take his share of the vacuum which the disappearance of Germany has created. But the economic picture cannot be separated from the political. There are two revolutions going on in Europe. The feudal countries of eastern

Europe rise toward industrial socialism. This revolution is in search of abundance, the material example of which is America. It is actually a revolution toward Americanization, but on a socialistic pattern. The industrialized countries of Western Europe are turning from capitalistic industrialism toward socialistic industrialism. This is a movement not toward abundance but toward the control of abundance. Sweden has progressed farthest in this revolution; the platform of the Swedish conservative party, made up mainly of the nobility and the industrialists, would read to some Americans like a leftist manifesto. So would the platforms of the Christian Democratic Party of Italy and Germany, the Christian Republican movement of France, and the Norwegian Christian Socialist Party, whose platform is (quote) "The Bible." In Europe these parties are rightist as against the socialist left. In this picture the Russian Revolution is already obsolete, for it forces the dynamic of an awakening people into the frame of a nineteenth century dogma and an eighteenth century police state.

Concerning Russia I found three views prevailing in Europe which I should like to call the black, the white, and the grey. They all center around the definition of the word democracy. In a recent poll conducted by the Swedish Gallup Institute concerning the meaning of the word "democracy" among the answers given were "right of the people to govern themselves," "same rights for all," "free press," "contrast to dictatorship," "like Sweden," etc. The bulk of the answers, however, 31%, was "Don't know." One wonders when seeing this result in a country like Sweden, what it would be like in this country or in some others of the United Nations. Democracy is impossible as long as people are ignorant of it. And, as Kant once stated a hundred and fifty years ago, without world-wide democracy peace itself is impossible.

In that same poll interesting answers were given concerning the countries which were to be regarded as democratic. From the black point of view, Russia was regarded the mortal enemy of Sweden and of all democracy. From the white viewpoint, Russia was seen as the prototype of a truly democratic society. The grey position saw Russia as neither the one nor the other, but in between those two extremes. Sweden's attitude toward Russia, like that of any European democracy, is naturally intimately connected with her attitude towards the United States. According to the "black" point of view the United States is the prototype of democracy, from the "white" position it is the last bastion of vanishing capitalism. From the "grey" viewpoint we are neither the one nor the other, but in between these two extremes. The Swedish people, as a whole, it seems to follow from the poll, tend to the black view rather than the white or the grey. The order of democracies, according to the percentage of their answers, is as follows.

95%	Sweden
86%	England
85%	USA
65%	Finland
59%	France
25%	Poland
14%	Russia
3%	Spain
2%	None of these.

As can be seen, Sweden tops the list, Russia and Spain end it. There was, according to my own experiences, no doubt in any Swede's mind that Sweden is the best working democracy—the five percent who did not think so thought that Russia was a better one because of its liquidation of "capitalists." I encountered however considerable discussion concerning the democratic status of Russia and the United States. The primaries in Mississippi and the lynchings in Georgia repelled some Swedes into stating that whatever our country was, it was not a democracy. On the other hand I met some Swedes who said that their own country might behave undemocratically if of its six million inhabitants six hundred thousand were Negroes. This, they added, would speak against the insufficiency of human, even of Swedish, nature rather than against the concept of democracy. Another argument against the democratic character of the United States related to the strikes paralyzing our economy.

Swedish economy has long since passed the age of nation-wide crippling strikes—the only strike going on while I was there was one of cinema operators, a sad state of affairs which prevented me from visiting the elegant Stockholm cinema salons. The blame for the strikes in this country was laid by most people with whom I spoke, on the stubbornness of the American employer rather than the intransigence of the American worker.

The fanaticism with which the profit motive is upheld in this country is foreign to the temperament of the Swedes. I sometimes heard the American workers blamed for their inability to educate their employers and to win political power. The American worker was called "primitive" and "narrow-mindedly economic." A good example of this view is the following passage from Stockholm's Aftontidningen under the heading "American Tragedy":

> In domestic politics America is without doubt far behind Europe, in spite of Hitler and Mussolini. The American labor movement is a typical example. The trade unions are very strong, as is evidenced by the result of the many strikes this year. The members of the trade unions represent almost a third of the total electorate, and even though Sweden in this respect has a head start the difference is not big. But whereas the Swedish workers have understood that they must first win political freedom and political power in order to realize their economic and cultural aims, America tries to take a short cut, an attempt which in the eyes of a European observer is bound to fail in the long run. Until CIO some years ago started PAC, their political action committee, the two great trade unions have been almost uninterested in political action. The strikes aim at higher wages and better working conditions, and the main aim of the workforce organizations is greater efficiency in their dealings with employers and rival unions. But the private capitalistic structure of society is taboo. In addition there are in many cases purely reactionary tendencies within the unions, some of them, for example, exclude Negroes from their ranks.

Another daily, Dagens Wyheter, brought out in July a long article entitled "Shocking Hate of Jews Among New York Germans" with reports of Yorkville conversations which would come as an eye-opener to many Americans. The admiration for this country is thus not uncritical in Sweden; but the majority of Swedes regard the United States as the flagbearer of democracy and the western way of life. They regret our shortcomings as unfortunate deficiencies of human nature which must be corrected but which do not spoil the picture as a whole. Most Swedes regard the existence of the United States as the one bright spot in the world picture. As one of them expressed it to me, the integration of a continent of forty-eight states into one free nation "is like a divine miracle." American history is regarded by many Swedes as the paradigm of democratic history and the lack of its teaching in Swedish school as a failure which must be remedied immediately.

On the other hand, more Europeans regard the materialism of our country and its lack of value in public life as the one sore spot which must either be overcome by a reformation of our standards of value or else it will spread through the whole body politic with disastrous results not only for this country, but for the whole world.

The reverse side of this attitude toward America is the European attitude toward Russia. The more sympathetic the attitude is toward the United States, the less sympathetic it is toward Russia, and vice versa. The Russian problem is the uppermost in the European mind, and the rest of the world is seen, so to speak, through the prism of that problem. In the 'black" view Russia is a gigantic potential danger and a threat to the democratic way of life. The "white" view, on the other hand, is that in spite, or perhaps because of, the dictatorship, a new culture and civilization is arising in Russia. This view I found in only a very few conversations. Most interesting was a Swedish author who asked me what I would say to a dictatorship in the state of Mississippi which forced the people to go to school, to wash regularly, to suppress all racial prejudices, which would put into prison all Bilbos and Rankins. Slightly more numerous were those who held to the "grey" view, seeing both sides of the Russian problem, the strides toward a better life for two hundred million people made by a determined leadership and, on the other hand, the unreality and isolation in which that same leadership was keeping those same people whom they are supposed to educate to reality.

Depending on whether the sense of facts or that of fiction would win out in the long run in Russia, these people held, Russia would become either the flag-bearer of a new civilization or the first victim in the definite collapse of the old. Russia, in this view, was like an overgrown adolescent, still unsure of its own vaguely felt powers and with all the delusions and clumsiness of her immaturity. "Let them grow up," a famous professor said to me. "Maturity, which came to us in four hundred years cannot come to Russia in twenty."

Russia is not yet mature—but what does this mean? Here we come, I think, to the most profound difference between Russia and the West, or rather between the eastern and western worlds. The difference is this: the eastern world, from the River Oder to the Japanese Sea, cannot think in terms of the individual. The individual as such does not mean anything in that world, he has meaning only as a representative of a half-mythical collectivity. To us, on the other hand, the individual means everything, and the collectivity has meaning only insofar as it is represented by valuable individuals. The collective, in these politically immature states, has not yet been tamed to serve the individual. Man is as yet of no value there, nor is humanity; only the State is significant. This is a primitive view, betraying the weakness of the individual who must lean against the mighty collective. This same view of the all-powerful collective is found in varying degrees throughout Europe, even, to a slight degree, in its democracies. It is the survival of the tribal in modern society. The dignity of the individual is in political practice, the great heritage of the Anglo-Saxon tradition, especially of England. In moral thought it is the heritage of Christianity and the Hebrew tradition.

Today we who are the products of this tradition are the ones who must be missionaries for human values all over the world, as against the tribal magic of the State. When in Nurnberg recently an unknown American soldier shot the chauffeur of a Russian general, American authorities searched for weeks for the culprit, without success. A friend of mine was charged with the disagreeable task of telling the Russian general that unfortunately we were not able to find the criminal but would make any indemnity he requested. The general looked in astonishment at my friend and said, "Oh, that matter! Well, never mind, I've got a new chauffeur."

Not socialism, communism, capitalism, nor any ism, not economic or military strategy holds inherently the key to the future of the world. Our hope now is that we shall be able to teach the world the true value of man. Only then shall we able to fill the word democracy with meaning. When I visited a Polish convalescent home the men told me of the last few days of their former existence when they weighed 60 and 70 pounds, were mere skeletons of their former serves, ridden with all kinds of disease, and how in this state they had marched one hundred and eighty miles before they were liberated. They marched with no clothing but old blankets, "our noses to the earth," as one of them expressed it, one step a minute. A German with a Red Cross armband and a pistol in his hand shot through the head anyone who slumped. They moved on; the road was covered with corpses like leaves in fall, they "moved," pestilence-stricken multitudes. "We had," they told me, "but one thought in our hearts: Freedom, Freedom. Thousands of American planes over us thundered the message of freedom. Every bomb, which sent the Germans cringing into holes, made us laugh. We just stood there and laughed." I asked them, "What gave you the power to go on?" "Just this," one man said, "the knowledge of the end. The goal was in sight. It was not a physical power which held us up, for our bodies were dead. It was moral power. We don't know whence it came to us. But it was there as long as we needed it."

The other men nodded. I looked at them, one after the other. I imagined the scene, the diseased skeletons moving wearily along the road to freedom, every step meaning life, every stumble death. Every minute meant the summoning of new energy into their shriveled bones. Whence did it come? What was man? Was it these shriveled bodies, or was it the source of seemingly inexhaustible energy from which they drew their strength? Finally, I asked, "Now tell me, what is Man?" No one answered. One of them finally, speaking in German with a Polish accent said, "ja, was ist ein Mensch—yes, what is a man?"

Man—it is the key word of the age to come. But it is a word that must be defined and made a working concept, capable of standing up against the tyrannies of states.

> A state? What is that? Well, open now your ears unto me, for now I will say unto you my word concerning the death of people. A state is called the coldest of monsters. Coldly lieth it also; and this lie creepeth from its mouth: 'I, the state, am the people.' It is a lie!... Confusion of language of good and evil; this sign I give unto you as the sign of the state. Verily, the will to death, indicateth this sign! Verily it beckoneth unto the preachers of death!

Thus spake Zarathustra, in the words of Friedrich Nietzsche. To the preachers of life beckons the sign of Man. Man the unbounded potentiality, Man the creature whose faith can move mountains and whose thought can lift the earth in its angles, Man the being who has conquered the power of the sun—he must now conquer and tame his own unbounded energies. If he succeeds there will be order and peace. If he fails there will be chaos and war. The talk about war is as childish as the talk of a boy who discusses whether he will get a spanking tomorrow. He definitely will if he does the misdeed. He definitely will not if he does not do it. It is entirely up to him. Mankind will definitely survive if it does the good, from now on. The good is the reformation of the animal which calls itself human today into the creature of God which is man.

This reformation is coming. Millions and millions of people in Europe are expecting it. They know the ways it must take. They have lived through the problems of man—through all of them. Above the political and economic trivialities which now occupy the world scene, most inspiring of all my experiences was to find in almost every man and woman I met, no matter how different their racial backgrounds, the longing for the new, the spiritual, the moral leadership. All we need is a man or men who will catalyze this world-wide longing into a workable synthesis. When I say there will be no war I say it because I feel as deeply as I have ever felt any truth, that such men will arise—not today, not tomorrow, but they are on the way. They will breathe new life into the moral skeletons who now move wearily along the road of civilization. They will do so simply by clarifying the goal for mankind, by organizing into clear, nay, scientific transparence the concept of man. Then the power which is Man will become actualized in the works of peace, and the spook of mechanical, materialistic, old-fashioned, and obsolete economic and pseudo-political totems will sink into the dust. Peace today is impossible—yes, it is, materialistically and even logically speaking. But precisely the impossible it is which this nation and other nations achieved during the war. With the help of God, with the determination of every one of us, and with the inspiration to come from a new prophet, Peace Will Prevail.

CHAPTER VI

The Challenge of Peace

EDITOR'S NOTE

Clearly, in this speech, Hartman struck a chord with listeners. He first delivered it at the Honors Day Convocation of Ohio State University on May 17, 1949. Then, he later delivered the same speech at a Convocation of Randolph-Macon College in Lynchburg, VA, on June 8, 1953. The speech also was subsequently published in the magazine, Vital Speeches of the Day and, later, in the Ohio State University Alumni Magazine on July 1, 1953.

If, upon reading, it sounds familiar, you will recognize that it was most likely edited from the lengthier and more scholarly essay, The Science of Peace, previously included as a chapter in this book. We decided to present in this collection both the written and the spoken versions of Hartman's message to demonstrate both the continuity in thought and the variety in expression of his corpus of work.

Hartman warns his audience that "What happened in Germany can happen to any nation. It is likely to happen if technological societies do not muster their moral energies." Despite such a warning, the speech offers an optimistic view of the future: Hartman declares, "By 1990 we should have peace and many of us will see the day."

———————

In speaking to you of peace I speak of course as a philosopher. Twenty-three hundred years ago a meeting of great consequence for the cause of peace took place in the house of a certain Caphalus in a suburb of Athens. Its subject was Peace and the Philosopher. One of the party, Socrates, told a parable, the most famous parable of the Pilot which you can now read in Plato's Republic, to illustrate the relation of the philosopher to the State.

There was once a ship, he said, the ship of state, rocking in the gale, thrown here and there in the dangerous straits, every minute in danger of crashing. The captain is a little deaf and has a similar infirmity in sight, and his knowledge of navigation is not much better. For there is no reliable method of selecting the captain. Instead of people doing what each is best fitted to do, the baker baking, the candlestick maker making candles, the haberdasher selling shirts, everybody thinks he can do anything, with the result that the baker makes candles, the candlestick maker sells shirts, and the haberdasher becomes president. Every Tom, Dick, and Harry thinks he can steer the ship and the sailors are quarreling with one another about the steering, everyone being of the opinion that he has a right to steer though he has never learned the art of navigation nor can he tell who taught him or when he learned. So they throng around the steering wheel, fighting each other, throwing each other overboard, killing each other with bottle-necks, strangling each other with red tape, and knocking each other groggy with all kinds of motions. In the meantime the ship is rolling crazily, always in danger of crashing on the rocks or against other ships.

But there is one man on board who takes no part in the universal chaos but sits in one corner, his legs drawn to his face, doing nothing but looking into the air. Everybody regards him as the ship's moron. Actually he is the only one who would be able to steer the ship for he is charting its course in the stars. This, of course, is the philosopher. So the meeting comes to this result concerning the question of Peace: There will be no peace on earth until the philosophers are statesmen, or the statesmen and rulers of this world have the spirit and power of philosophy. Until that time the cities will never rest from their evils, nor will the human race.

This was twenty-three hundred years ago. Since then the cities have never rested from their evils nor has the human race. So it is time, perhaps, to let the philosopher have a try at peace.

Already peace is recognized as a psychological problem, in the preamble of the constitution of the United Nations Educational and Scientific Organization, which says that wars begin in the minds of men and it is there that the defenses of Peace must be constructed. This, we might say, is halfway on the road to philosophy, considering, the definition of a philosopher: the one the psychiatrists go to.

There was a time when Peace was a religious command from on high, chanted by angels "Glory to God in the highest and on earth peace, goodwill toward men." Today peace is a matter of life and death. To put it crudely, it is a matter of whether you and I shall live out a normal life or be blown sky-high "before our time." Peace today is a pragmatic necessity. We have to bring it down to earth as a practical task.

In doing so, however, we shall, by necessity, lift up the whole level of earthly existence. The Son of Man who was born under the chant of angels on Peace said that he had come so that we may live and live abundantly. The time has come to fulfill these words. We shall either die or live abundantly. There is no middle course. And it must be our generation that shall not pass before these things are done. What follows is to be a method of peace as a practical task for us to fulfill.

What we need is very simple. We need a new Spirit. We need a new Science. We need a new Method.

We need a new spirit. Some of us don't know it yet, but this is a great time to be alive. It is the greatest time humanity has ever experienced. First of all we must get the contagion of the greatness of our time. Cynicism and confusion are as out of place today as they were in the great time of the Renaissance. They are signs of weakness. This is no time to be weak. As in the Renaissance, mankind is embarking today on a new and fantastic adventure—its third great venture: the moral unification of the world.

It took the whole of history so far to unify the world in body and mind and now we must unify it in spirit. To be exact, counting history from the beginnings of Egypt about 4000 years before Christ, it took fifty-five hundred years to unify the world in body, and five hundred years to unify her in mind. If the ratio keeps on in the same proportion it will take forty-five years to unify the world in spirit and bring about peace—just about one generation, yours and mine. By 1990 we should have peace and many of us will see the day.

98

Two consecutive ventures integrated the world's body and mind. Before Columbus the body of the world did not exist for mankind. There were at least three worlds, mutually unknown to one another, and even undreamed of: The European, the Asiatic, the American. Each of these worlds had its empires and beliefs, and there was less conscious intercommunication between all three than there is today between the planet Mars and this earth. Mars is an object of continuous observation and interpretation; America was not even imagined. Columbus, venturing into the dark unknown of the ocean, fearing to be blown off the terrestrial disk with every new blast of wind, triumphantly proved the roundness and wholeness of the earth. Though he did not reach the Indies he opened the gates through which later Magellan, Drake and other circumnavigators could safely travel.

When the earth was known man turned toward his second great task. This time he did not venture into new realms of the earth but new regions of the universe. He plied the dark ocean of space, not with ships that carried his body but with telescopes and spectroscopes that carried his sight. He advanced into the unknown land of electronics, of chemistry, of molecular and nuclear physics. His scientific discoveries contracted and integrated the physical body of the earth. Today the world is one. It is as big as ever, but small in comparison with man. Man's body and mind have outgrown the earth. He is virtually omnipresent; his voice can be heard—and soon his picture seen—at one and the same moment all over the globe. His mind can communicate with every other mind on earth in a flash. His body can move around the globe in less time than it used to take to traverse a large city. Man's body and mind span the earth.

Man integrated the body of the world, in the geographical revolution of Columbus. He integrated the mind of the world, in the scientific revolution from Copernicus to Einstein. He must now integrate the con-science of the world. This is the moral Revolution of our time. Instead of delving into and ordering the chaos of material nature man must now delve into and order the chaos of his own nature. Thus we need, secondly, a new science.

We have to bring ourselves up to date. We are living in two ages. With our emotions we are still in the Stone Age, hating and loving, envying and desiring as primitively as the cave man; with our intellect we are projecting planetary travel. Our political institutions are rooted in the eighteenth century and some of our so-called modern societies use devices of classical tyranny if not tribal cannibalism—yet, we build the atomic plants of the next century. We have learned to control nature before we have learned to control ourselves. In doing so we have lost control even of our own inventions and have thus magnified our chaotic emotions to global if not cosmic dimensions. We have made our world a monstrosity, mixing the noiseless efficiency of techniques with the groaning of tortured men and women. We suffer from moral schizophrenia. Man, in the words of a philosopher, is a rope stretched between the beast and superman. One more tug, and the rope will snap; the superman will revert to beasts. To one society this has already happened.

What happened to the Germans can happen to any nation. It is likely to happen if technological societies do not muster their moral energies. As it is, our moral and social life lacks intelligent organization.

In the coming fiscal year our federal government will spend twenty thousand million dollars for the armed forces. Included in this sum are one thousand million dollars for so called "basic research"—scientists who will be busy to find better ways of destruction, financed by an annual budget which exceeds all the assets of all American foundations. These scientists, busy for the armed forces, will not do research into the minds of men where, according to the preamble of UNESCO, the defense of Peace must be constructed, but into the properties of matter. Yet, the same armed forces had to reject four and a half million men for mental and physical disorders, one and a third million for mental disorders alone. These men were indicative of a minimum of 14.5 million Americans suffering from mental disorders on any given day. Every year 125,000 new mental cases are admitted to public hospitals alone. Almost 70% of all public hospital beds are occupied by mental and nervous patients. For research into this problem Congress, in the National Mental Health Act, appropriated the expenditure of seven and a half million dollars—one fortieth of one percent of the present war budget and three fourths of one percent of the appropriations for war research.

The ratio should be reversed.

The ramparts of peace are healthy minds in healthy bodies. Rejection for war service is one measurement of personal fitness. Rejection for peace is another. This measurement is applied by society which admits or rejects individuals according to their mental and physical fitness. Rejection by society is not yet regarded as a sign of illness. It is regarded as "bad luck" or "failure"—and failure to "make the grade" or to live a happy life is not regarded as a sign of abnormality. "It can happen to you and me," we say, it is "normal." Normalcy is regarded as the average state of affairs, and that state, we are resigned, is rather bad.

However, normality as the average state of affairs within a certain group is relative normality only; it is relevant only to that particular group. In a group of morons the moronic is the "normal." In addition to relative or average normality there is absolute normality. Absolute normality is the state of Peace.

The requirements of peace are infinitely higher than those of war; rejection for peace is more wide-spread than rejection for war. For this reason it appears more "normal." But "average" individuals are not sufficient to keep the peace. If peace is the normal, then normalcy is more than the average. Measured by the standard of efficiency in keeping peace, humanity is today, and has always been, subnormal or abnormal. It has always been able to conduct war thoroughly; it has never been able to conduct peace. The 4-F's of war felt a sting of conscience; we are all 4-F's of peace, but it doesn't bother us.

War is a show of machines, peace one of men. We are good at war for we know machines and can handle them. We fall short in peace for we don't yet know men nor how to handle them. Our society rejects men at an appalling rate; it turns out misfits, neurotics and criminals by the millions—rejectees of peace. Such men become aggressors in war. War is the escape of social misfits from normalcy. The abnormality of war is their natural element. When World War I broke out the social misfit Hitler felt "as though saved from the annoying emotions of my youth. Overwhelmed by stormy enthusiasm I sank to my knees and thanked God from the bottom of my full heart." For World War II he was able to thank himself. In Hitler we found the epitome of all misfits of peace. Such misfits are able to wage war but, as Air Marshall Tedder has expressed it, "they know war from A to about Y." They lack the final insight into the course of events. They are able to convert peace into war, normality into abnormality, but are unable to reverse the process, to convert war into peace. The paradox of war lies in its being abnormal only as long as it is not actually begun—for once all nations are embroiled in war everything becomes abnormal and hence the abnormal becomes the normal. This is the reason an aggressor nation always scores its success at the beginning of a war when there are still traces of normalcy left and the normal minds have not yet "caught on." But once, in total war the abnormal has become the normal, the minds of normal men—the attacked rather than the attackers—work more efficiently. They apply, so to speak, the logic of peace to war and thus are at an advantage, for the final end of war is peace. Therefore aggressors always have failed in the long run, and in the last war the "boys who wanted nothing but go home" did go home, on their own terms. Aggressors fail by the very dialectic of their abnormal minds. Their final end is war, and in war they remain, unable to survive into the era of peace. To attack in an era of global war implies defeat. To the degree that the minds of men are unfit for peace they are also unfit for war. Research into the minds of men is therefore as urgent a task for the nations as research into the properties of matter.

Research into the minds of men would enable us to construct the defenses of peace. It would show us the subtle deviations from normalcy which spell both insanity and its colossal counterpart, war. We may call these deviations moral illness.

Moral illness is beyond the point at which normalcy ends, just within the realm of abnormality, in the tensions of everyday life, our quarrels and disagreements, maladjustments and frustrations, prejudices and delusions. It is with moral illness that wars begin. In the words of a recent writer, "we have the roots of war in the home, the church, the school, in every family disagreement, in every church row, in every frustration, every maladjustment, every dislike, every jealousy, even in bad humor and bad luck. All these symptoms of strife and tension, in all people, can grow together like the boils of a plague, to form one ghastly eruption. The ethical teachers of mankind have always seen war in this comprehensive light, as the sum total of all situations of strife.

On the other side of the line is the realm of normalcy, the world of appreciation and cooperation, enjoyment and satisfaction, open mindedness and imagination, in a world, the world of peace. Its roots, too, are found in all situations of life, in home and church and school and business. Peace is the sum total of all situations of cooperation. Cooperation, for sane people, is the norm.

In order to find the point at which cooperation breaks up in tension, normalcy passes into abnormality, we must discover the minimum conditions of both normalcy and abnormality. To this end we cannot study abnormal phenomena, for here normalcy has already crossed the border line. We must study normal phenomena and follow their transition. Only thus can we find out at which points social and moral health passes into social and moral illness, and peace assumes the symptoms of war.

When plants are retarded in growth we know how to cure them; agricultural research stations dot the land, federal funds are appropriated by the millions for research relating to soil and erosion, the growth of trees and orchards. But there is no ethical research station, doing investigation into the soil of morality, the growth of man and his body and mind.

Without such research all other research is futile. Even the research into war would be in vain, for it is research into the conduct of a disease rather than its cure and prevention. "Basic research" today ought to be research into the minds of men. The question of such research ought to be not: how does nature work? But: how good is man? What we need is a science of Ethics.

Just as the natural sciences have developed from the vagueness of commonplace conjecture to precise disciplines, so ethics must develop from commonplace conjecture to scientific precision. Its obvious categories, like good and evil, right and wrong, virtue and vice, self, value, freedom, choice, person, must be analyzed—and will probably lose in the process the fundamental importance present day ethics ascribes to them—just as the obvious categories of nature, sound, color, shape, and the like, have lost their fundamental importance in the natural sciences. In these sciences patterns and configurations of waves and vibrations, electrons and protons have, as primary qualities, replaced the sensuous secondary qualities of things. Similarly we shall have to penetrate to the primary qualities of moral reality.

The natural sciences have developed methods which have brought gigantic natural powers within the reach of any individual able to turn a switch or push a button. Similarly ethics will have to develop methods which will bring the moral powers of man within the reach of every individual. There will never be a moral push button, but there must be moral expertness.

A hundred years ago we were ignorant of the nature of electricity. The research of men such as Faraday, Maxwell, and Hertz clarified the exact nature of that power. The genius of practical inventors like Marconi and Edison brought it within the reach of every man.

Today we are ignorant of the nature of moral power. Theoretical research workers must define and analyze the power of man as it appears in the intricacies of human behavior. The genius of practical researchers must apply this knowledge to the management of individual and social affairs.

Thus, thirdly, we need a new method—that of integrating all sciences over the common denominator of man. Man is the giant who lives on the level of the atom and on that of the stars. The science of man cuts across all the lines of scientific and even of metaphysical division. Like the decimals of irrational numbers to fill the gap between the integers, so hyphenated sciences must be used to fill the gaps between the sciences—not only bio-physics and biochemistry, but also psychophysics, psychobiology, social psychology, medical economics, psychosomatic medicine, social ecology, mathematical geography, genetic ethics (gen-ethics) bio ethics, zoological ethics, physical ethics, ethical physiology, ethical etymology (two sciences projected by Nietzsche), ethical musicology (projected by Plato), cosmic ecology and even, as suggested by Schopenhauer, cosmic demography.

The integration of the sciences over the common denominator of Man will bring about a new insight which must open the narrow divisions of custom to the vision of a moral universe. As the men of the Renaissance began the building of the natural sciences on which our technological society is founded so the pioneers of ethical science must build the foundations of the moral society of the future. In another generation, as we have today colleges of Arts and Sciences, of Horticulture and Pharmacy, of Engineering and Dentistry, so we shall have colleges of Ethics. Eventually everybody will be able to apply to every life situation moral standards and scientific insight.

Thus, we would lay the theoretical foundations for a better world. We would add to the space-time world the moral dimension. We would bring about the reformation by which the world of technical science would become the world of moral conscience.

Between the good of tomorrow and the evil of today stands the ignorance of man about himself. If only a fraction of the research funds used for the preparation of war would be used for research into the conditions of peace the chances of man's survival would be immeasurably strengthened. What we need in this research are not so much instruments or techniques as Thought. The old Platonic prescription still holds. The moral future is among us but it cannot be reached through the patent office. It must start from within. Its aim must be the glory of man in all his creative power and cooperative achievement.

CHAPTER VII

How to Beat Communism

EDITOR'S NOTE

Having completed the report of Hartman's 1946 trip to Europe, we jump in time to approximately 1951. During the intervening post-war years, the Cold War had risen to prominence as the number one issue in international politics.

Hartman's essay, "How to Beat Communism" is written as a Memorandum—a memorandum to whom, we do not know. It is written in a tone and style and length similar to his earlier "How to Win the Peace", which was addressed to Congressman Sol Bloom, chair of the House Foreign Relations Committee, some eight years earlier. This memorandum would not have been addressed to Congressman Bloom, as he had died two years before.

In his youth, Hartman was an ardent student of the writings of Karl Marx. His knowledge of Marxist thought is evident in this essay and is vividly documented in his 1958 manuscript, "A Partnership of Capital and Labor" which was published in German, but not in English.

An important thing to notice here is that—unlike Hartman's earlier writings wherein Hartman felt that the only way to defeat Nazism was through the military defeat of the Nazi party—here he argues that Communism can be defeated, not by military strength, but by understanding—understanding of philosophy and of social action. He calls here for "an adequate philosophy of human values and a program of global action."

If we want to beat Communism, we must know what it is and how it came to be what it is. In particular, we must understand that a power as tremendous as Communism which now encompasses one-third of the human race and seven hundred million people cannot be attacked by emotionalism, but only by expert knowledge of its causes and effects. What we need is a scientific approach. Just as we scientifically approach problems in technology or medicine, etc., so we must scientifically approach this problem of society.

HOW COMMUNISM CAME ABOUT

Communism is probably the most successful political movement in the history of the world. Its global reach today was achieved within a hundred years. But a hundred years ago, when the Communist Manifesto appeared, Communism was only the outpouring of two young students dissatisfied with the state of the world, living in an idyllic German cathedral city. What has given this movement the power to envelop the world? If we want to beat this movement and replace it with something better, we must know the mechanics of movements of global success. There are three steps in the development of Communism, as there are in the development of any successful social movement. They are: (1) A detailed philosophy which analyzes the present conditions and sets the goal in detail. (2) A movement consisting of readers and followers of the philosophy who elaborate the details and prepare its realization in action. (3) Social actions which bring about the reality of the philosophy.

The Philosophy

The philosophy must have all the attributes which make it penetrate the human mind and attract to it the thoughts of men. If it is true, as the Preamble to the United Nations' Educational and Scientific Organization states, that wars begin in the minds of people, and it is there that the ramparts of peace must be constructed, then this is even more true of Communism. It is in the minds of people that Communism begins and it is there that the ramparts of democracy must be constructed.

The attributes of a philosophy that can attract the minds of people must be three. First, it must be part of a stream of tradition and not be fetched out of the blue sky. Secondly, it must analyze in detail and in scientific terms the existing conditions so that the reader not only feels that he is reading the truth, but also that he is reading the truth in a particularly clear and creative manner, and thirdly, it must be positive and show a way out of the present situation, so that every reader feels inspired and enabled to do something to change the conditions described.

In order to create such a philosophy, there must be a man whose job for many years is nothing but thinking and elaborating the philosophy, until finally the full-grown work emerges into the world. The work which created Communism was Marx's *Capital*, which appeared in the years 1867 to 1894, twenty to fifty years after the *Communist Manifesto*. Year after year, Marx sat in the British Museum in London, writing—his friend Engels helping to pay his bills. The result was a philosophy which had all the attributes mentioned above to change the world.

It was part of a tradition, and not fetched from the blue sky. Communism is the child of European philosophy and economic theory. Philosophically, it is based on the work of Hegel, whose philosophy goes back on the one hand to 600 B.C., the work of Heraclitus, and on the other hand to Immanuel Kant, whose philosophy in turn is based on that of the English philosophers Locke, Berkeley, and Hume, the French philosophers Descartes and Rousseau, and the German philosophers Leibniz and Wolff. Marx's economic theories go back to the classical economists, Adam Smith and Ricardo. Ricardo's theory itself is based on the population studies of the English parson's son Malthus, whose work also inspired Darwin to his study of evolution. Communism, therefore, is not so much a perversion of the human mind, but a logical result of Western thought. It is the child of a century which believed in mechanism and materialism as the salvation of the world. It is a philosophy of the nineteenth century, and we must make it obsolete in the twentieth.

Marx's philosophy foresaw that the gap between proletarians on the one side and capitalists on the other side would, by the iron laws of economics and population pressure, become so deep that the ultimate solution could only be a revolution of the proletarians who had nothing to lose but their chains. He envisioned a capitalism developed to its culmination, with a large majority of the people as proletarians. The revolution that would be brought about by the proletarians would therefore be a dictatorship not of a minority but of a majority. In other words, it would be a "democratic dictatorship." This philosophy of Karl Marx became significantly altered by the works of Lenin and Stalin, who were bringing about the Communist revolution, not in a country of highly developed capitalism, but an agricultural and half-feudal country, namely Russia. Hence, Lenin had to change the Marxian thesis that Communism was possible only in a capitalistic country, and had to maintain that it could be established in an agricultural country and that the phase of capitalism could be leaped over. In such a case, however, there would not be a majority of proletarians, but only a small minority—since there was not yet of course an industrial society—and this implied the dictatorship of a minority rather than a majority, and became a despotic government.

The result of Lenin's modifications of Marx's philosophy is the fact that the present system in Russia is not Communism in the sense of Marx, but rather a system of state capitalism, similar to the one which in the countries of Europe preceded capitalism under the name of mercantilism. Mao Tse Tung in China is in this sense a better Marxist—and not a Leninist—since he proposes first to build up capitalism in China in order then, with the help of a proletarian which at present is not existing, to establish true Communism.

Stalin further modified the original philosophy of Marx by not only upholding the Leninist autocratic nature of Communist government, but even abolishing the international character of the movement—which under Marx and Lenin had the slogan of "Proletarians of All Countries, Unite"—and making it into a national movement, the slogan of which may be said to be "Proletarians of All Countries, Unite for Russia." This Stalinist modification gave rise to Trotskyism and Titoism and will eventually help to bring about the downfall of Communism.

The difference between Stalin, Tito, and Mao Tse Tung stems therefore from the Leninist and Stalinist modifications of the original Marxian philosophy. Mao Tse Tung may be said to be a Marxist, Tito a Leninist, and Stalin, of course, a Stalinist. There are, therefore, tremendous springs of explosion in these various Communist movements.

The philosophy of Communism as developed by all three of its prophets has in common two important features which add to the vulnerability of Communism, namely (a) disregard of the human person and (b) dogmatism. The disregard for the human individual is a disregard of the human mind and of the supremacy of the human spirit, and springs from the glorification of circumstances, environment and other materialistic conditions. The Communists do not understand that within the mind of each person is an unlimited power, and that one spirited man can be worth more than an army of a million robots. What Communism needs is "masses," what Democracy needs is men—individual persons. This disregard of the human personality led Communism then to manipulate human beings and cross off their personalities as if they were just so many bodies. It is the principle of democratic philosophy, on the very contrary, that a healthy society can only be based on the free and responsible consent of free individuals. The Communist robots will, in a situation of serious competition, be pushovers for an organized democracy.

The second feature making for the vulnerability of Communism is their dogmatism. All facts are contorted into constructions that will fit them into the Communist dogma. This has led to the ridiculous falsifications of history, for example, that all Western inventions were made by the Russians or that America was discovered by them—of all things, in the year 1648! In the words of the new head of Prague University, a Mr. Mukarovsky: "It is dangerous"—listen to this peculiar remark of the head of a university—"to leave any fact, determined by impartial science, uninvestigated." In this way, Russian science is twisted and made sterile, just as are the biological experiments of Lysenko, and the issues of war and peace, democracy, and international relations are falsified.

This dogma has put the Russian people into a straitjacket, and already a crisis is brewing in the people. Some of their fliers desert, some of their officials leap out of windows, and many of their soldiers, who have seen Europe, are being sent to Siberia in order not to contaminate the Russian people, eager as they are to break the Iron Curtain. Here again, combustible material is right at hand for us to light. Yet, these faults of Communist philosophy and practice have not yet seriously impaired its luster in the eyes of the world's restless peoples.

The Communist philosophy is a scientific structure, giving a detailed analysis of the situation, the laws of economics and indeed of the universe, and being capable, for minds with not too high ambitions and yet a scientific bent, to fill out their entire life and all of their activities. The study of the Communist writings and the sciences of economics, history and psychology built on them, is a challenging task for any man. It is the only philosophy of society, so far, which has been shown to be workable by scientific manipulation of society. The Communists are, so far, the only social engineers, and they have applied the mechanical designs of the nineteenth century to society. The result is a science of inhuman relations. An equally earnest and detailed method must be devised for a science of human relations, built on true human values and the powers of the human spirit.

The Communist philosophy is positive and gives a detailed method of political action. It was elaborated, not only in the writings of political leaders, but also in actual experiments, such as the revolution of the Commune in Paris of 1870 and the revolution in Russia of 1905. Today it has become a veritable school for revolutionaries and in the Soviet Encyclopedia Stalin gives his occupation as "professional revolutionary."

- The Movement. Communism has become, through the attributes of its philosophy, a world movement within a century, or, if we count from the appearance of Marx's Capital, within three-fourths of a century. This movement is penetrating more and more into the minds of people, and will do so as long as it is not countered by an equally effective philosophy and a program of action which promises a new society and at the same time eliminates the conditions of want, poverty, and ignorance on which Communism thrives.
- Because Communism has become the greatest coordinated movement of social action in the history of the world, having behind it not only generations of eager zealots, but also, absolutely unique in the history of the world, the entire resources of a nation of two hundred million people in the potentially richest land on earth.

How can this power be matched?

The Movement to Counter Communism

It can be matched only by a philosophy equally clear, detailed and powerful, by the full resources of another nation, and by the equally devoted work of social reformers and political experts. This counter-philosophy must be based on the very opposite values from those of Communism, not on matter but on spirit, not on bodies but on minds, not on the power of things but on the power of personality. This philosophy can only come from the American people, who already in physical and material power counterbalance Russia and the Communist world, but who at this moment have not yet developed an adequate philosophy of human values and a program of global action. American science and philosophy have made this country great. How can they transform the world?

How the Power of American Democracy Came About

America has become great by the same process that all other movements have become great, namely, a philosophy, experiments, and action. The power of American democracy is based on two philosophic streams, one highly elaborated and directive, the other more vague and experimental. The first is the philosophy of technological society, the second is the philosophy of democracy. The former has all the attributes of a globally successful philosophy. The latter has to be elaborated by us in order to become equally effective, as a science of human values capable not only to withstand but to supersede Communism.

The Rise of Technology

The rise of technology was due to a philosophy which was detailed, logical, experimentally verifiable and hence could be realized by men of action, engineers, architects, designers, laborers. The philosopher on whose work this technological world was built is Descartes, who as a young man of twenty-three, in two dreams in November, 1619, conceived of the combination of the sciences of algebra and geometry and thus created in analytic geometry the basis of modern mathematics. He proclaimed this tool as the universal tool of all science, and his successors, Newton and others, built on his foundations the science and technology of modern times. In the last instance, the technological marvels of our time, on which is based the power of American democracy, go back to the dreams of Descartes. In mathematics our engineers and investors, architects and laborers, have the universal frame of reference needed for the solution of their problems and the realization of their own dreams of mechanical wonders in planes, trains, bridges, motors, dams, and tubes, pipes, cranes and whatnot. This mathematical frame of reference is now bringing about a global technological society, and even the Russians have to use this tool created by Western philosophers. It is quite logical, therefore, that they would proclaim it as their own invention.

The Rise of Democracy

Thus we have a perfect philosophy for a technological power. For the organization of our society, however, we do not have an equally detailed theory. We are basing our institutions on the thoughts of men such as Locke and Montesquieu, who admirably developed social philosophy for the eighteenth century and gave Jefferson and the fathers of the American Constitution the intellectual tools for building the institutional framework of this great country. This framework has lasted for one hundred seventy-five years, and even though it was designed for an agricultural people of no more than four million, has become, by continuous experimentation in trial and error, the valid foundation for the highest industrialized people on earth with a population of one hundred fifty million. What is needed now is an elaboration of the social philosophy of democracy, so that it will be applicable, not only to America, but to the whole world, and not only for a highly industrialized country like ours, but also for the still undeveloped feudal and agricultural countries of the East. In this way, the wind could be taken out of the sails of Communist propaganda, which at present is the only one which seems to give a promise for a better life to the world's undeveloped peoples.

The philosophy which we must develop must have all the attributes of a globally effective philosophy. It must be detailed and scientific—a science of human values. This science of values must be as definite as is the science of mathematics, and it must be to the social sciences as mathematics is to the natural sciences. Instead of vainly and dilettantically going in all directions in social affairs, politics, and diplomacy, we would then have a science that would show us in detail where to go and when, what to do and how in each situation, precisely as Communism is a science of this nature. This science of human values must be based on the supremacy of the human individual and the human conscience. Our philosophers are now working on such a science; their efforts should be enlisted in accomplishing it in the soonest possible time. In this way democracy will have an intellectual weapon of the highest caliber to direct its efforts to conquer the minds of the world's peoples. What Marx says in *Capital* that "the proletarian finds in philosophy its intellectual weapon" must be even more true in democracy. Its intellectual weapon must be the philosophy of value. An Institute of Research in Values should be established at once with the cooperation of professional philosophers in the field, a body of scientific rules and norms of values should be developed and a curriculum worked out for a College of Ethics which should be established as a nucleus for all people of good will who want to act in a socially effective way. This college would serve as a pilot plant for similar colleges all over the country, and indeed, all over the world. Just as the Manhattan Project condensed into a few years a process which otherwise would have taken decades, so this project, by a concentrated effort, could condense into a few years what otherwise would take decades. It would bring about a globally effective philosophy not, as in Communism, in a century, but in less than a decade.

This philosophy being developed and alumni of these colleges being ready to go into the world, a movement of global proportions would exist, and political experts of moral action could go out into all nations to preach and practice the science of human relations, based on the values of individual people. Such a movement would come like a liberating stroke to all the peoples of the world who now in intellectual despair are reaching for Communism—only to find that Communism is not interested in people. Our movement on the other hand would show not only that the individual is the center of social life, but it would also design the institutions by which the individuals in all countries would be able to develop themselves. The greatest power on earth is the good will and decency in the heart of each human being. We would touch the heart of each man and liberate his best potentialities; we would make him subservient not to a state or a nation, but to his Maker himself. It would be a movement that would put into practice by the means of scientific analysis and engineering, that is, of a socially effective action, the meaning of the Gospel and fulfill the sentence in the recent statement of the Conference on The Responsibility of Christians in an Inter-dependent Economic World, convened by thirty-two Protestant denominations in Detroit: "Christian religious principles must be translated into concrete measures, expressive of the Christian religious idea. This is a task for stewards whose engineering genius, executive ability and research skills are regarded as a sacred trust. Scientific means must be discovered with which to realize moral ends."

116

Such a movement of democratic missionaries, prophets, and moral experts all over the world, would develop means, not only of economic assistance, rehabilitation and development of backward areas as is now envisaged on a modest scale in president Truman's four-point program, but it would use all the resources of this nation to preach, practice and spread the gospel and institutions of freedom to all peoples. It would be a mobilization for freedom; not "total diplomacy" but total morality.

The Institute to be established would work out a detailed program of such action. An investment now of only a few million dollars in such activity would, in the long run be an insurance against war, death, and the waste of life, as against spending billions, as now spent for annihilation.

CHAPTER VIII
The Secretary of Peace

EDITOR'S NOTE

The exact date when this paper was written is unknown. From its context, we can conclude that, most likely, it was written between 1951 and 1953. Nor is the audience for this paper made clear from either the document, itself, or from surrounding papers found so far in the Archives.

This paper is important in that it is the first expression of Hartman's developing thoughts about the end of sovereignty. He argues here, as he will argue even more forcefully in subsequent chapters, that because of nuclear weapons and instant worldwide communications, the role of the nation-state as sovereign over the affairs of humankind must come to an end. He writes that, "Today the alternative is either death or abundant life—there is no middle course."

And yet, he recognizes that the situation in the world is not yet ready for his vision of "a new life of peace, worthy of and suitable to the American way of life."

So, in this document, he spells out a temporary middle course. The middle course that he prescribes calls for a Cabinet-level position known as The Secretary of Peace, whose mission, to the extent possible, is to offset and counter-balance those of the Secretaries of State and Defense. Further, he states, this office will be required as long as sovereignty remains the dominant operating theory of world governance. It is a necessary waypoint, so long as some countries remain totalitarian. For, in Hartman's mind, a world-wide civil society, based on morality rather than on military strength, can become a reality only if democracy is spread worldwide, and totalitarianism, in all its forms, is erased.

Hartman writes here of what he calls the "collectivistic fallacy." The collectivist fallacy is the fictitious notion that a nation-state—any nation—is a collective reality rather than

*a composite of individuals. He calls this notion of collectiv-
ity the disease of sovereignty. Here Hartman harkens back
to a metaphor he used in "The Triumph of Gravitation." He
writes, "We flatten out the people in collectivist terms...."*

*Hartman's stated goal in this essay is to "convert internation-
al relations into inter-human relations, relations between
nations into relations between people." A Secretary of Peace is
his recommendation for a next-step in that direction.*

**"Things which have never yet been done can only be done by
means which have never yet been tried."**

— FRANCIS BACON

We are today engaged in a cold war with Russia and a hot war with
China. We are acting and being acted upon, as nations have since the
beginning of history, namely, as organizations of physical power. Our
leadership in Washington, both Government and Congress in complete
unison, are engaged in building up our power and in producing what
Secretary of State Dean Acheson has called "situations of strength" in a
course of action which he calls "total diplomacy."

There is no reason why this policy should not lead where such policy
has always led, namely to total war. There is no reason why in the field of
politics the laws of logic should not hold which hold in all other fields of
life. Just as little as one can learn by being lazy, lose weight by over-eat-
ing, stay sober by drinking, be happy by suffering, say the truth by lying,
or survive by committing suicide, in a word, achieve an end by doing its
opposite—as little can one bring about peace by arming for war.

If we want peace, and there is no sane person who does not, we
must prepare for peace. We must break the vicious circle into which the
necessity of the present situation has forced us and attempt to break
out of it by changing the situation and the climate of the world, from
one of war to one of peace. We must stop playing the game of our
enemies and letting ourselves be dragged down to their level, morally,

physically, and politically, forced to play a role which is foreign to us by tradition and temperament. Instead of playing the game of power politics, of "total diplomacy", we should lift the international discussion to the level of morality; instead of letting our living standard be dragged down to that of the undeveloped nations and letting our resources be sapped in futile pursuit of physical force, we should build the world up to our standard; instead of forcing our political life into the totalitarian strait-jacket of government controls, we should liberate the totalitarian peoples from their own controls. We should take the offensive for a new life of peace, worthy of and suitable to the American way of life. Instead, we are in the process of tearing up this way of life, rather than leading the world along the path of freedom we are being dragged along by Russia on the path to destruction. Russia may be behind an iron curtain; she has forged around us much more tightly an iron ring of necessity out of which we do not seem to be able to extricate ourselves. The following program is one that will get us out of this vicious circle of power politics and instead of making the world totalitarian will make it free. It will overcome the evil rampant today with good. It will substitute total power by total intelligence, total diplomacy by total morality, total destruction by total life.

Today the alternative is either death or abundant life—there is no middle course. Thus Peace, which in the gospel is nothing but a promise, a glorious suggestion from on high, chanted by angels at Christ's birth, is today a pragmatic necessity. And Christ's coming, which was to make us live and live abundantly, must either be vindicated, or the world will perish. We not only have cosmic power; we are in a cosmic situation. Nations today are blind monsters, standing opposed to each other, as the apostle saw them, in mortal fear and murderous intention. We must convert them into free organizations of fearless, creative, humble, and fully living human beings.

The task is not as difficult as it sounds. We have all the conditions for success. By Providence the role of making the world live is given to us in America. All we have to do is to translate the great heart of America into dynamic action.

I shall first trace the roots of the present evil and then design its cure.

The situation of power in which we are caught today stems, historically, from the institution of sovereignty. Sovereignty was originally the attribute of the absolute monarch who was the founder of the nation state, and it became, without any change, transferred to republics after the abolition of absolute monarchies. There is no difference in international relations between the sovereignty of an absolute, totalitarian nation such as Russia, and a democratic nation, such as the United States, a constitutional monarchy such as England, or an absolute monarchy, such as in Iran or Saudi Arabia. Sovereignty in all these cases is the same, namely, the fiction that a nation as such is beyond the law. This essential immorality of sovereignty is well illustrated in the 29th chapter of Thomas Hobbes' Leviathan, the classic treatise on the origin of the nation state. Hobbes there speaks of the six "things that weaken, or tend to the dissolution of a commonwealth," the six "diseases of a commonwealth" or "doctrines repugnant to civil society." These diseases of an absolutist commonwealth are precisely those attributes which today constitute the foundations of democracy. They were called by Hobbes diseases of the absolute commonwealth, and rightly so, for what is health to democracy is death to absolutism. These six features are: 1)limitation of power in the sovereign, 2) moral independence of each private person, his being a judge of good and evil, 3) obligation to follow one's conscience and regard anything done against conscience as sin 4) subjection of the sovereign under the civil law, 5) private property as excluding the sovereign, 6) division of power. For Hobbes these were vicious doctrines and their very opposite was necessary for a strong sovereign state. The power of the sovereign must be unlimited, he alone is to be judge of good and evil, individual conscience has no moral significance, the sovereign is beyond the law, all property is subject to seizure by the sovereign, he is law giver, judge, and executioner all in one. The Hobbesian commonwealth was a totalitarian state, in our present terminology, and the fact that national sovereignty arose as essential property of such a state makes it clear that from the point of view of democracy the origins of national sovereignty are immoral.

Diplomacy, which is the realm of the Secretary of State in our government, is the arm of sovereignty. It is necessary in a world of sovereign nations. Moving in the realm of sovereignty, it moves in the realm of immorality. According to Webster, diplomacy is the "art and practice of conducting negotiations between nations; artful management in securing advantages without arousing hostility." According to Talleyrand, a more authoritative source, it is the art of using your tongue in order to conceal your thoughts. For Clausewitz, diplomacy is the intellectual dimension of war, and war the extension of diplomacy. Total diplomacy, Mr. Acheson's phrase, is the method of waging the cold war. Total morality would be the method of waging peace.

The very features that made sovereignty immoral were accepted by sovereign states, including democracies, in international relations. Too little power is abhorrent to any sovereign nation in international affairs. Nations are not people, but powers, "Great Powers" as we say when thinking not of the people of America, England, Russia, but of collective abstractions, "U.S.A." "Great Britain," "U.S.S.R.". Power politics is the lifeblood of total diplomacy, or rather its death blood, for in seeing abstractions total diplomacy disregards people. In its field of vision are only collective bodies, nations, and the individuals of these nations come into focus only as so-called manpower, in the last analysis as appendages of war machines, useful only for pulling triggers. In the words of one great Frenchman, Jean-Paul Sartre, who is appalled at the collectivistic trend in present-day American thought, "The moment that you cease to regard us as soldiers you will rediscover us as friends." These people are not our friends now because they see that we are not interested in friends. Friends are individual people. We are not interested in people as individuals. We are interested in nations as powers. Therefore, we are not interested in what the people of other lands think, feel or desire. We see them as military allies or enemies, and their lands as strategic bases or targets. Thus we send an ambassador to Spain, not because we are interested in the happiness of the Spaniards, but, in the words of an editorial in the Ohio State Journal of December 29, 1950, because we "want to get Spain into the Western defense setup." Spain, for us is not a people, but a strategic base, "by the gate of Mediterranean, supplied with good seaports and landing fields and 28,000,000 inhabitants, could be a valuable defense partner."

Thus we look at people as tools, in the same category as seaports and landing fields, and end up in military thinking, the natural culmination of the philosophy of total diplomacy and the sovereign state—with war in the spirit. Thus we think of Formosa, Indo-China, and other places where people live, as strategic bases for United States power, and of countries actually as weapons. Formosa, in MacArthur's mind, is nothing but an unsinkable aircraft carrier. We ourselves are nothing but tools. In the words of a well-informed writer in Life magazine of January 3, 1951, "in our total defense planning we must strike a calculated balance between the preservation of essential people and essential machines.... In a nation such as ours, where the individual life has always been regarded as the most precious thing extant, it will be difficult for our people to grasp this new scale of values. How would anyone like to be told... that a turret lathe is more precious to the country than he is?"

This scale of values is of course not new but has been the scale of all power nations since the beginning of history. It is the scale against which Jesus rebelled, the scale of immorality and inhumanity. It is also, as history teaches, the scale of futility. For in disregarding people we not only degrade ourselves but neglect our best allies, namely, precisely the people of the earth and particularly the people of the dictatorships, especially the Russian people. The Russians are by and large as anxious, and more anxious, to throw off the yoke of dictatorship as we are for them to do so. If only we could see people behind the names of nation states our policy would become positive, creative, and moral. The military thinking of total diplomacy, in using people as machines and disregarding their humanity and individuality is not only immoral and un-Christian, it is also unreal and unintelligent. For, people being what they are, created in the image of God, and the world being what it is, the creation of a good God, the moral, the intelligent and the real go hand in hand, as do the immoral, the unintelligent and the unreal. The immoral therefore, in the last instance always ends in unreality, that is destruction. The so-called realists usually waste lives thoughtless of the true nature of the real world.

The second feature of absolutism is also prevalent in international relations. It is abhorrent to any nation that any other nation, or any body of other nations, should be a judge of good and evil. No, only my sovereign judgment is morality: "My country, right or wrong!"

So also with the other absolutist features. There is no moral conscience in international relations and no sovereign nation will subject itself under law unless it pleases her. There is no private property which can exclude my nation in international affairs. If my nation needs "military bases" it goes and gets them, either by diplomacy, that is power-backed persuasion, or simply by power. If my country needs raw materials or wants to keep colonies it does the same. All the Atlantic nations on the

European side of the ocean are more or less desperately resolved colonial powers, as the recent incident with the ruler of Bechuanaland [today Botswana], Seretse Khame, showed so dramatically when he married a white queen. Lewis Carroll could have written a nice parody on this, "Attlee in Wonderland"—the wonderland of sovereignty.

Finally, there is, of course, no division of powers of a sovereign nation in relations to other nations. In foreign affairs it is always true what is true for totalitarian nations: "Ein Reich, ein Volk, ein Führer!" one nation, one people, one leader. No internal dimension is ever allowed to erupt into the outside world, as Henry Wallace and James Byrne found out when they voiced disagreement with the Chief Executive.

What is bad in all these doctrines is the fiction of the nation as a collective reality and the neglect of the individual—the collectivistic fallacy. At the basis of it is mechanistic thinking, thinking in terms of physical power, which regards nations not as people but as power machines to be manipulated by social, political, and military engineers. This is the thinking of the leaders in the nation states, no matter whether these states are communistic, socialistic, republican, democratic or monarchistic. It is a disease of sovereignty. It brings it about that a mild and innocuous little man from Kansas City, who would never dream even of hurting the hair on the head of a cocker spaniel, orders as one of his first acts of office after becoming president of a large country, the incineration in a blast of fire of 80,000 men, women and children. Without any qualms of conscience, you and I would probably have done the same. Leading a nation we lose the reality of people. We flatten out the people of the world in collectivistic terms; instead of the home of the free, the land of the brave, the shelter of the poor, the opportunity for the rich, the place where love and compassion move human hearts, we see the world as a mechanical body inhabited by power constellations.

The final result of these collectivistic abstractions are distinctions not only of nations but even of individuals in collectivistic terms; they now lose their individuality and are regarded as representative of "isms", "communist," 'socialist," "imperialist," "interventionist," "isolationist." Thus they become labeled as either white or black, good or bad, or simply as animals, as were the Chinese in a recent cover of Time which showed them as grasshoppers. Such abstractionism leads to dogmatism, and many who believe themselves to be fierce fighters against totalitarianism are actually themselves totalitarians. Thus, instead of overcoming evil by good, namely dogmatism by information, and collectivism by appreciation of individuals, evil is raised to the second power.

So far the roots of the evil. Now let us construct the cure. First by diagnosis of the facts.

The facts are, first, that nations cannot be labeled as either good or bad. Secondly, that nations are not contemporary but each lives in its own historical time. And, thirdly, that nations are not collectives but people.

Nations are not just good or bad, communistic or capitalistic, but all shades and degrees. We have today two opposing political and two opposing economic creeds; on the political level, dictatorship and democracy, on the economic level, socialism and capitalism. Already these are generalizations, but they give rise to four different combinations which can again be combined among themselves into an infinite number of shades and degrees of political organization. If we combine dictatorship with socialism, meaning by socialism a planned economy, we get communism, the system of Soviet Russia. If we combine dictatorship with capitalism, we get fascism, as we have it in Spain and Argentina. If we combine democracy with socialism we get social democracy, the system of England and in a lesser degree, of the Scandinavian countries. If we combine democracy with capitalism we get the system of free enterprise of the United States. But actually none of these systems exists in purity. There are many capitalistic features in socialism and even in communism, such as for instance competition in a degree not even imagined in our society, and vast differences of wealth—only that the rich people are of a different kind than the rich people in our society. On the other hand, there are totalitarian features in a capitalistic democracy, such as the present total government control over the economy and the total control of some businesses, unions, colleges, newspapers, by one person.

Secondly, we must consider that nations are not contemporary but live in their own historical time, so that labels lose additionally a great deal of their meaning. People are contemporary only in bodies, but not in minds. Russia is today where Europe was around 1600 when there had never been a democracy in the large nations of France and England, when the state owned and operated the entire economic life, when workers were controlled and directed to labor and, if they did not do the labor assigned, were put to compulsory work in the salt and coal mines, when they had to have passports if they wanted to move from one place to another and were not allowed without such passports to move farther than one or two miles. In comparing the labor laws of Russia today and of France, England and Germany around 1600, one is struck by the almost literal agreement of the texts. The same is the case when one compares the art, literature and politics of those times, the coarseness and crudeness of expressions, faces, political methods. Looking at China one is struck by the similarity of the life of a Chinese peasant of today and the life of a European peasant in the feudal age of 1300 when there was sometimes not more than one pair of pants in a family, so that only one at a time could go out, when animals and men lived together in the same room, periodic famines and pestilence swept the countries, and the people had to eat bark and drink mud—as the Chinese often have to do today (unless there is an Army truck around, in which case they drink the oil in the crank case). Throughout these ages Europe was swept by uprisings and revolutions, almost all without success. Up to the French Revolution of 1789 there was politically no regard whatsoever for the individual person—as little as there is today in Russia and China. From a Marxist point of view, which presupposes a highly developed capitalism as predecessor of communism, there is no Communism in either Russia or China. Russia is in the period of state capitalism, much the same as was France under Colbert. China is in a feudal revolution, the revolutions of 1525, 1776, 1789, 1917 all rolled into one.

All this is mirrored in the metamorphosis of the term Communism. To Marx Communism meant the next step after a highly developed capitalism and, skilled as he was in the dialectic of Hegel it was, of course, impossible for him to envisage that a stage in the dialectical course of history could be leaped over. According to Marx, capitalism would develop—and he wrote one hundred years ago at the beginning of English capitalism—into a condition where a small minority would control all the wealth of society in a concentration of monopolies and the great mass of the people, the proletarians, would be impoverished and eventually overthrow the system which exploited them, in the revolution of the proletariat. The proletarians would then inaugurate their own communistic system in a dictatorship of the proletariat, which, however, since the proletarians were the large majority of the people, would be what is called democracy. Lenin changed this Marxian vision, for he had to deal not with a country of highly developed capitalism but a half-feudal agricultural country, Russia. According to Lenin it was not necessary for a country to be completely capitalistic in order to become communistic, but it could leap without intermediary steps from the pre-capitalistic into the communistic stage. This was, of course, heresy from the point of view of Karl Marx. Lenin's statement implied that the dictatorship of the proletariat would have to be a real dictatorship because there would be no majority of proletarians since there was no antecedent developed capitalism. Stalin further narrowed down the so-called communism of Lenin and made it not only dictatorial but even nationalistic, thus further modifying the Marxist slogan, "Proletarians of all nations unite!" It was this narrowing down of communism which Trotski objected to as a betrayal of the ideal of world revolution.

Thus today we have various kinds of "communists". Tito, seeing the state capitalism of Soviet Russia is a Marxist, yet in building up his own dictatorship he is a Leninist in regarding Stalin as a national imperialist he is Trotskyist, yet, in furthering his own nationalism he is a Stalinist. Mao Tse Tung, in first trying to build up a socialistic democracy based on the peasantry seems to be a Marxist, yet, in doing so as a national dictator he cannot help but be a Leninist. There is a good chance that, given encouragement of independence from abroad, he will develop into a Titoist. But to disregard his revolution and pin one's hope on the incompetent and defeated Chiang Kai-shek is another example of the ostrich-like unrealism of the so-called realists—who are actually worse than ostriches, for ostriches only disregard reality whereas these "realists" add to disregard of facts wishful thinking. They are political romanticists.

The common denominator in all these developments is that neither Russia nor China nor the other undeveloped peoples have ever had democracy and are living in a different historical age from ours. Unless we understand this we shall continue to flounder from mistake to mistake. Instead of acting like one of these undeveloped power boys we should act as mature leaders and teachers and with wisdom and example lead them along the road to democracy. But a whip has never yet been a good instrument of education, nor has a bomb.

Nations, finally, are not "nations" at all. A "nation" is a collective abstraction as is a "corporation." Like a corporation, a nation is people.

As Paul G. Hoffman, former head of E.C.A. [Economic Cooperation Administration, which administered the Marshall Plan] said recently, "We have this strong conviction—derived from two years involvement in this 'cold war'—that the first thing to do is to start thinking in terms of people, stop thinking in terms of governments or countries. There are 270 million people in Europe." And there are 800 million people in Asia. As David Lawrence said in an editorial in the United States News and World Report of December 29, 1950:

> We need to examine the status of peoples rather than the status of governments who claim to represent them. Our primary obligation is to humanity—to the innocent peoples who are the victims of governments that seek to exploit people and make cannon fodder of their youth. Once we have the courage to make this differentiation— to make the case clear to all peoples—the road becomes clear.... We compromise with truth, we appease, we bargain with evil when we try to deal across the table with tyrannical and despotic governments.... We must have a bold policy that applies first the great instruments of moral force—renunciation of evil governments.

This is the program. This course would convert international relations into inter-human relations, relations between nations into relations between people. The supreme value would be the human individual—he alone would be the total, the inviolable "sovereign." Between people no diplomacy is necessary, as little as it is necessary between the non-sovereign bodies of corporations in a sales contract, or between two cities or two states within the United States. All that is necessary here is morality and civil law.

A world community of this sort would be one which lives under world government. But world government is a formal goal which must be given a material content and a method by which to reach it. The content of world government is the moral world community living under civil law. World government is possible only as world democracy, as was emphasized by Immanuel Kant in his essay On Eternal Peace, in 1795.It is impossible in a world with totalitarian governments. Such governments would make not only the existence but also the realization of world government impossible. Russia, for one, would never join it. Without Russia a "world government" would be one of two armed camps, just as the present "United" Nations are really two armed camps. In order to bring about genuine world government the world must be rid of totalitarianism. Waging national war against totalitarian nations is no solution for two reasons. On the one hand the free nations would go totalitarian in the process and on the other hand, the war would not be waged against the real enemies of humanity, the totalitarian governments, but against their innocent victims, the enslaved peoples. The only solution is a bold program of ridding the world of totalitarianism. This is a step preliminary to the formation of world government without which world government is impossible. It is a stage of transition which has not been sufficiently considered in the discussion on world government.

The first point on the program must be an extension of the concept of war. War exists whenever a government attacks either the peoples of other countries or its own people, that is to say whenever a government moves against the expressed will of its people. Any totalitarian government, whether of the left or of the right, must be regarded as at war with its own people.

This necessitates a new agency in the Federal Government and eventually in all governments of the world. Whereas the Secretary of State has to smile to outrage and smilingly outrage, there is no agency or government department set up to deal with peoples and to appeal to peoples, not only over but, if necessary, against the heads of their governments. This would be a Federal Department not hamstrung by the necessity of playing power politics, or of being "diplomatic," but an agency concerned exclusively with the weal and woe of men and women all over the world. This agency would have one moral standard; it would regard as good everything which helps and furthers the development of individuals and as evil everything which hinders and obstructs individual growth. It would be the political dimension of morality. It would speak the language not of diplomacy but of morality. It would be the Department of Peace of the United States of America. It would realize and fulfill the moral destiny of this nation. Its various functions would flow from the fact of the supremacy of the human individual and the needs and opportunities of his development. It would be the catalyst of cooperation among men.

For the Secretary of Peace, what is important in foreign lands would not be material things such as oil and ore, but the people. Therefore our policy toward other peoples, say Arabs, would be very different from what it is now. At this moment we regard Arabs as appendages to oil wells and as pawns in a strategic game against the Soviet Union. We do not care, nor are we interested in, how an individual Arab peasant lives; we are only interested in the material resources of his soil and the strategic position of his country against Russia.

A Secretary of Peace would be interested exclusively in the personal welfare of the peoples of these regions. He would have the power to help improve their standards of living, their education and health. He would be in charge of Point 4. He would foster commerce, agriculture, industry, communications, and the arts of these peoples. He would put the strength of his country behind the social, economic, and cultural programs of the United Nations, just as the Secretary of Defense puts strength behind the United Nation's military efforts. In a word, the Secretary of Peace would extend all the functions of a native govern-ment for the welfare of its own people to people in foreign lands.

This implies secondly, that the Secretary of Peace, in seeing peoples and not governments, would take a firm stand against any oppres-sion, colonial and otherwise, and for the freedom of individual peoples anywhere on earth. At present, paradoxically, it is Russia which has this position in the eyes of many peoples on earth; the more oppressed and hence desperate and ignorant they are the more they follow the Russian line. As long as Russia helps and aids their economic demands in their own countries, these people are not interested in the misery of the Russians themselves. Why should they? As Jean-Paul Sartre says in the article I mentioned, "the Communists everywhere defend the exploited and oppressed—though they feel free to abandon them if Russian interest demands it. To this you answer, and you are right, that in Russia there is a concentration-camp government. But what do starving Korean peasants care about the Russian penal system? Or even under-nourished French workers, when their just strike is being supported by the Communist Party?" And what of American aid, when America's Marshall subsidies are channeled to enrich the men against whom these workers are striking? To them America and Russia look different from what they do to us. All this, of course, is a sad perversion of truth and result of American bungling, which the Department of Peace would rectify. Actually the natural leaders of the oppressed of the earth is the country which first liberated itself from absolute colonial government: The United States of America. The Secretary of Peace of the United States of America would speak with the voice of the American revolution for the moral revolution of the twentieth century.

The third implication of this new organization of international politics is the necessity of our strength; and here I mean physical strength as long as evil governments are in power. The Secretary of State and the Secretary of Defense will have to continue to deal with the old-fashioned power aspect of nations as long as there are governments which are, or are potentially, at war. For, as Churchill rightly said in his speech in Fulton, Missouri, the dictatorships, particularly the Russian, fear our friendship more than our hate—our friendship, namely, for their subjected peoples. There is nothing Stalin—and for that matter Franco and other dictators—fear as much as their own peoples. They are not afraid of the atomic bomb, as long as they are sure their peoples will support them in throwing one back—but they are afraid and mortally so—of the home-made bomb that one disgruntled subject might throw into the path of their armored car. They have the streets blocked off by military police when they pass through town, they have their food pre-tested—there is no more powerful ally for us than the subjected peoples of dictatorships. The dictators' power is their hold over their people—there, and only there, is their Achilles heel. What makes them so powerful and dangerous is the strength of their peoples—they themselves are just small human beings. They draw power from the brawn and brains of their peoples. Take this power, the minds and support of their people away from the dictators and their power crumbles to the dust. The first dictatorship to fall must be the Russian.

This then is the Program, to be spaced in three steps: First, the President of the United States is to proclaim our new policy. Second, Congress is to institute and the president to nominate the Secretary of Peace. Already this will have tremendous repercussions throughout the World. Third, the President is to declare that a state of war exists between the Soviet Government and the Russian people and that the full strength of the United States is allied to the Russian people. The Secretary of Peace will implement the Presidential Declaration. He will mobilize the genius of America, its technology, communications, transportation, advertising, to reach the Russian people and help their liberation from dictatorship. What the Russians need is not weapons—all they need is knowledge, constant encouragement and support. They will do the rest. We will parachute to them the goods of civilization, radios—as suggested by the President of RCA—tractors, automobiles, watches, candies, nylons, the whole arsenal of the good life. We will show them that industrial production, which they are being driven to in slavery, has been achieved by America a hundredfold in freedom, and that we are willing to share it with them.

Then, finally, we will have extricated ourselves from the iron ring forged around us by the dictators, we will wage the fight on our own ground, and for the first time the dictators will be stumped and stunned. How can they suppress such action? How can they deny brotherhood manifested day in and day out not in words but deeds? Shall they mobilize their secret police to round up the American automobiles that drift in on balloons from the sky? How will they drown out the hundreds of small and large radio stations which the Secretary of Peace will operate all around the globe? Shall they confiscate the little American radios which we have dropped to their people? Destroy the tractors we have sent? How will they find the films and projectors we have flown over? Will they take away the candies which the children are eating? How will they fight nylon underwear? Haven't they promised their people the good life? Here it is—coming to them on the wings of friendship. And what will all this cost us per year? Less than a few battleships and much less than an atomic bomb. But it will release a chain reaction all over the earth.

The danger will then be that the dictators, like cornered beasts, will try to break out with the only means at their disposal, namely physical force, both against their people and us. In this case we will have to float over to the peoples weapons. For this emergency we have to retain and maintain our Defense establishment. But in this case the war will be a just one, the oppressed peoples will be on our side, and our motives will not be judged as they are now as just another kind of power politics.

To bring this about no miracle is needed nor any Utopian faith. All that is needed is boldness and organization—the very essence of American enterprise. We are now considering building a satellite to the earth. This is a project of the Pentagon at this moment, subsidized by tens of millions of our tax dollars. Instead of such fantastic schemes, let us organize the peoples of the earth for peace in a program of action.

In this way, and in this way alone we will fulfill our mission. In this way alone we will bring about peace rather than war. Only this way will we have the great earth peopled with men and women in the full enjoyment of their power, living abundantly the new life which is the only life that can be lived from now on. On this positive aim we must concentrate our energies, not on war. All else is perversion—concentration not on the bodies and minds of people but on their corpses. Bold, dynamic, pioneering, this is what the hour demands. We have to fulfill our promise to mankind. Today, more truly than when Lincoln spoke, we shall either nobly save or meanly lose, the last, best hope on earth.

CHAPTER IX
The Revolution Against War

EDITOR'S NOTE

Hartman's essay "The Revolution Against War" was a long time in development. It began, apparently, as a speech entitled "Our Existential Situation: We Will All Die Together." Where, when, and whether this speech was delivered, we do not know.

It was expanded and re-titled, and subsequently published as the closing chapter in a book entitled, The Critique of War: Contemporary Philosophical Explorations, *edited by Robert Ginsberg, published in 1969 by Henry Regnery Company.*

It is re-printed here with permission of Regnery.

This somber essay marks a significant shift in Hartman's thinking about war and peace. In an earlier essay in this volume, "The Science of Peace", what he only suggested, once the time is ripe, he calls for boldly here. That is, he calls for the end of national sovereignty.

Hartman writes, "War,' said Clausewitz, 'is the pursuit of national goals by force.' It is obvious that we cannot speak any more of war, for national goals cannot be pursued by nuclear weapons....It is therefore nonsensical to speak of nuclear war. There is only nuclear-world destruction. The notion of war is not usable anymore."

The Cuban Missile Crisis of 1962 had a profound, existential impact on Hartman's thinking of matters of war and peace. He repeats here the experience he and Rita had of driving through Mexico and Texas on the way to see their newly born grandchild for the first time, when they learned on the radio of President Kennedy's address to the nation on the brink of war.

Hartman's warnings are increasingly valuable to those of us living in the 21st century. He wrote: "If ever a madman, such as Hitler, came to power in a nuclear nation, he would only have to push a button in order to have his boldest dreams of chaos surpassed by mad reality."

As Hartman puts it, "national defense" is no longer a valid idea. Peace is no longer a matter of weaponry. It's a matter of morality.

This essay deserves a careful reading and thoughtful consideration. As difficult as it is to dwell upon the prospect of nuclear destruction, it is a topic we should not ignore. Hartman offers us a way to avoid the path to destruction.

———————

It seems paradox, but both the times of war and of peace are behind us. The time of war is behind us, for what threatens the human race is not war but extinction. War, according to Clausewitz, is the pursuit of national goals by force. National goals cannot be pursued by nuclear weapons which wipe out all nations. War thus has become self-contradictory, a self-contradiction epitomized in the already classic words: "It became necessary to destroy the town to save it." As the time of war so the time of peace is behind us. What lies ahead—if anything does—is not the opposite of war, peace, but the opposite of Death—Life. To rid humanity of war there must be a new awareness, almost an explosion, of man's will to live. There must be an existential awakening.

Of the three riders of the Apocalypse—Pestilence, Famine and War—the first is a natural evil to be overcome, and being overcome, by natural science. The second is partly a natural, partly a social evil, to be overcome, and being overcome, by both natural science (revolutionary agricultural techniques) and social revolution. The third is a purely human evil, created by man, to be overcome by a revolution of man's own self-awareness, a moral revolution which must produce a new man, sensitive to the immorality of war and not deceived by the slogans used to justify it.

Even now this revolution is on the way. Mankind is revolting against, and revolted by, war as never before in history. The reason is in part technological—television has brought the horrors of war into the living room—and in part moral. There is an awakening to the futility of violence in general, and an understanding of the suicidal nature of nuclear violence in particular. There is an awareness that the life of mankind, its existence, is in the balance. The revolution against war thus is an existential revolution, born out of the anxiety for the life of man on earth.

The natural dangers of life, even its social dangers, are being contained by powerful ramparts of human organization, especially the State. But the state is a gigantic Dr. Jekyll and Mr. Hyde. While it is a fortress against natural and social evil it is at the same time the creator of human evil. While the Department of Health, Education and Welfare develops ingenious means for prolonging life on earth the Department of Defense, with the same ingenuity, develops the means for its destruction. While the Department of Agriculture advises farmers on how to improve their livestock the Pentagon kills 6,000 sheep in a slight change of wind laden with nerve gas.

This poses a clear lesson: we have to develop the civil department of the State while getting rid of the military. We have to kill Mr. Hyde and help along Dr. Jekyll; and we must be more successful than Stevenson's hero. We must, first of all, learn clearly to distinguish between those of the State's features which are beneficial and those which are detrimental; between the state as an administrative unit and the state as "sovereign", as supreme ruler of our lives and deaths, and above the moral law. We must learn to understand that while the civil function of the state is legitimate its military function is illegitimate. If the state is to grow today it must do so intensively, not extensively, qualitatively, not quantitatively. In the first sense it is the servant of the people and its welfare, in the second it is the manipulator of its life and death. The latter is the function of sovereignty. Secreted away in the landscape and cityscape of the nation are the instruments of war, and among their peaceful citizens walk those who serve these machines. The combination of men and machines of the Sovereign State is the most powerful complex in the world. It is geared to Death; and it can turn everything state and society stand for to ashes in the wink of an eye. It is a vehicle of catastrophe. Thus, the second thing we must be clear about is this: as long as the State continues its sovereign function we are living under the shadow of instant catastrophe. Our life is poised on a sword's tip. The old Socratic word that the unexamined life is not worth living is literally true today. Unless we examine this precarious life of ours we may lose it at any moment, and such a life is not worth living.

The Greek word "catastrophe" means "sudden turn"; the sudden turn which ends everything. Only in few situations are we conscious of the possibility of catastrophe, as in an airplane. Sometimes, as in the Greek tragedy, we see the noose of fate being tied slowly, knot by knot, and although we see with clear eyes the threatening fate we feel powerless to escape it. Generally, however, we live without the presentiment of catastrophe. Our life goes its tranquil course—or at least we think it does.

Actually, we are too busy with the tasks of everyday life to have either the time or desire to reflect on what a shaky base rests our daily life; how finely all its elements are balanced, how exactly the earth must circle around the sun, how precisely the currents of air and water, how sun and rain, and the whole of nature must keep itself in balance to make possible our existence. A little more heat and we burn up, a little colder and we freeze to death, a small fissure in the crust of the earth and we fall into the abyss and our houses bury us, as recently happened in Sicily and Yugoslavia.

All these are natural risks of our existence. We all unite in order to prevent such disasters or, if they happen, to soften their impact. The State is nothing but an insurance company which mobilizes the means of all in order to help those in misfortune. We all pay the policeman at the street corner in the hope that we shall never need him, just as we pay our insurance premiums in the hope never to have to claim them. We are happy when our money profits others. As it was written on some of the houses in my village in Bavaria: "Saint Florian, protect our town, pass by my house, burn others down." (*Oh heiliger Sankt Florian, verschon' mein Haus, zünd and're an.*) We want to have nothing to do with disaster, we leave it to the others. We recognize its possibility theoretically and protect ourselves routinely. We leave its coming to statistics and are convinced that it does not concern us. Our own life is well ordered, somehow protected, we believe, through the rationality which, thank God, is inherent in the world and the course of our own life. We take the good times as our due and are desperate when misfortune hits instead of being grateful for every minute of happiness. We believe that our life is safe. In this belief rests our security and our happiness.

Suppose now we would start with the thought that our existence is precarious, uncertain and every happy moment an unexpected present. In this case we would not take the everyday occurrences of life as matters of course. Our whole life would take on a new dimension, one of gratitude toward a kind fate or God or a power which watches over us and protects us against evil. We would not only live but experience every moment; we would be aware continuously of the limits that are set to our existence. We would perceive our existence as a limit situation in the sense that every moment could be the last—although, thank God, it is not. Limit situations, say the existential philosophers, are situations in which man collides with the inevitable, final and inexplorable limits of his being—guilt, death, fate, chance. In such situations we become conscious of our own existence—which otherwise we take for granted—and all our values take on a different hue. Our whole life, as a limit situation, would be under the species of eternity—in the consciousness of the infinity which surrounds our own finiteness.

When we ask people what they think is the main thing in their lives we get all kinds of answers. Knowledge, love, money, success, health, but rarely the answer which is existentially the only correct one: the main thing of my life is that I live it. The fact that I am, that I was born, brought into this world. This substance of our existence we forget and are content with some qualities of this existence, money, love, success, etc.; but all these are possible only under the condition that I AM. If I am not all these qualities and gifts are not either. Qualities of existence are only possible when there is existence itself. Therefore, to concentrate on qualities and forget the substance which alone can have these qualities means concentrating on the inessential and forgetting the essential. He who lives a life that forgets existence and concentrates not on life itself but its accessories does not truly live; in the existential sense he vegetates. Instead of living, as the existential philosophers say, he is merely around, he has not life but Dasein, being there, being thrown into this world by chance. And when he dies he has nothing contributed to the world. He will, after a longer or shorter presence here, simply disappear, eliminated from the world, so to speak, as indigestible; for the world is one large organism which is being existentially nourished by those who truly live. If such nourishment through true living does not take place, if people are just around, like things, then the world itself dies off. We call this degeneration, decadence, decline; and historically it has happened to all civilizations, Egypt, Greece, Rome—and it may now be happening to us.

It is therefore not a matter of indifference how we live; for our true life is a contribution to the life of all. If we are not concerned about our own selves we neglect not only ourselves, but we neglect in ourselves all others. If we do not love ourselves, says Jesus, we cannot love our neighbors either; and if, says Kant, we neglect humanity in ourselves we neglect humanity in all.

At the times of Jesus and Kant these admonitions were just as true as they are today; but they were not of vital necessity in the sense that my neglect of myself could mean literally the death of all my fellowmen, of my own family, my children and children's children. I could neglect myself and waste my life and yet not immediately drag down the whole world with me. The welfare and misery of my fellowmen was not immediately dependent upon my own spiritual wellbeing—except if I was a leader of peoples, a general or a politician whose moods and caprices could lead thousands and millions into misery and disaster. And even in such situations the individual had always the possibility of avoiding the disaster. As Hegel has said, the juggernaut of history destroys only those who don't get out of the way. Almost the entire population of North America consists of the offspring of those who got out of the way of the juggernaut of European history. The human situation, in other words, up to now never was a limit situation. What was limited were the catastrophes; and even though there often were some sudden turns, through natural or historical powers, even though often hundreds of thousands, indeed millions, had to die together, even though their individual death, the most private act there is for each of us, was a spectacle of collective powers, there have always been places on this globe where the quiet, well thought-out plan of daily life, the sequence of day and night, the rhythm of the seasons went its balanced course, through the months and years, and where men, women and children could live their daily lives for three and four score of years.

All this has now ended. All of us are in a limit situation in which we depend so much one on the other that, if we do not all see the existential dimension of our situation, we shall all die together. As in the Greek tragedy the fates are spinning the thread and, turn by turn, are entwining us in the web. And, as in the tragedy, were are all either too blind to see the unavoidable fate is being prepared for us, or, if we see it, too powerless to avert it. Unlike the persons of the Greek drama, however, we are not the creations of a poet; we make the drama ourselves. We are ourselves the poets of our fate. And with open eyes and hearts we could, through our own action, ward off the disaster and turn what threatens to be catastrophe into abundant life.

THE COSMIC RANGE OF THE STATE

The catastrophe which threatens to engulf us is due to a well-defined shortcoming of man, an incapacity of organization which philosophers for two and a half millennia have clearly seen. Unfortunately, philosophers have never yet had the power to do anything about it. They have never been able to influence the State, our insurance against disaster which prepares our disaster. Socrates' words in the Republic are as true today as they were then: "Unless either the philosophers are kings in the states or the rulers of the states have the spirit and insight of philosophers, and thus both coincide, the power in the state and philosophy, there will be no end to the misfortunes of the states nor, I believe, of the human race." States, says Plato, must be built on dikaiosyne—justice, as it is often translated. A better translation would be "correctness," for dike means correct judgment. States must be built on correctness; and correctness, in the Platonic definition, means everyone doing his own. Everyone should dedicate himself to one activity in the service of the state, to that, namely to which he is best suited. Unfortunately, and that is the core of the evil which overtakes states, the most important places in the state are occupied by those who are least capable to fill them. The reason for the misfortune of states, says Plato, is that two types of persons are wrongly placed, the politicians and the philosophers. The politicians are people with small thoughts in big situations and the philosophers are people with big thoughts in small situations. The education of the philosopher-statesmen, or statesmen-philosopher, is the solution of this unhappy situation. It puts the man with big thoughts into the big situation and the man with small thoughts into the small situation. In the transposition of these two types and their places in the state lies the necessity of catastrophe. This is the moral of the parable of the pilot.

The ship of state is being thrown hither and yon on the waves of the sea, between the rocks of the narrows, the whirlpools of the deep, and there is nobody who can steer it. The captain is taller and fatter than the rest of the crew, but somewhat deaf and nearsighted, and equally defective in the art of navigation. The sailors fight for the wheel, each of them thinking he can steer the ship although he has never learned the art of navigation and cannot name a master who could have taught him. Indeed, they proclaim that the art of navigation cannot be learned on principles, and tear to pieces everyone who says the opposite. They fight among themselves, fetter each other in red tape, hit each other over the head with bottlenecks, throw each other overboard, overpower the captain with beer and wine, tear the steering wheel out of his hand, plunder the stores, and make the trip a wild orgy. The ship groans and creaks and desperately ploughs its way through the waves; until it founders on the rocks and sinks into the deep. There is only one man aboard who is unconcerned about it all. He sits in a corner, his knees pulled up to his chin, looking up into the sky. Nobody bothers about him and he is regarded the ship's fool. He is the philosopher. He is the only one who could steer the ship, for he studies its course in the stars. He is the Pilot.

The whole gigantic work of Plato consists in inventing methods by which the philosopher could take the wheel of the state, and in planning the education the philosopher must have for this purpose. It makes nice reading; and a hundred generations have had their pleasure with it while the politicians were busy ruining the states. Not one state since antiquity has lasted until today. One after another has gone down in the waves of history. Today humanity itself faces extinction. The world situation has become so big that politics and philosophy cannot be separated anymore. The politician, in order not to see his state annihilated, must be a philosopher; and the philosopher, in order not to allow his politicians to annihilate him, must be a statesman. The inventions of the natural philosophers, from Galileo to Einstein, have produced weapons which do not stop at the borders of their own states or of those of their enemy states; they expand over the whole world of mankind. We are all, not legally, but actually, members of one single community, linked together in one common fate, for life. For the situation of the philosopher, the universe itself, has become the situation of the state—and thus that of the politician. This situation up to now, had been limited to small states, from the Greek polis to the City of Rome and its empire, which still was only a small part of the world, to the feudal rules and the national states, still only fragments of humanity. All these forms of states are today fused into a unity, a comm-unity, linked together for better and for worse. and for death.

In this new situation the old organization of states and nations is obsolete. We have to think in new categories. The sanction for our failure to do so is that we will all die together, in the collision of nations with which our own state may have nothing in common except that it exists on the same earth with them. The whole earth in its course around the sun is the new ship of state. Who can and should steer it? Where is the stellar map that charts the political course of the planet? What is the accident which may cause the death of all of us, and how can it be avoided?

Plato's solution was fundamentally simple and easy to realize. But nobody took it seriously. The Athenian cities, the Roman so-called empire, the feudal and the national states, all were too small to recognize the necessity of the philosopher-statesman. But today it is obvious that the situation is so tremendous that it cannot be mastered any more by politicians. During the Cuban crisis Kennedy and Khrushchev wrote each other letters actually imploring the other to restrain himself and not lose control of the situation. The situation was in imminent danger of getting out of their control. They were both at the terrible threshold of catastrophe when the rational is being overtaken by the irrational, the horrible situation of the pilot who suddenly feels his plane does not obey him and uncontrolled, an object of gravitation, is crashing to earth. In natural catastrophes it is the force of natural gravitation which brings the disaster. In artificial situations, as those of the state, it is the force of artificial gravitation which brings the disaster. The total situation of artificial gravitation is war. It transforms everything into throwing and falling, makes the whole machinery of the state a gigantic sling-shot, a catapult of projectiles and grenades, fires and gases. Into this machinery Kennedy and Khrushchev saw their state disintegrate. It was in the process of slipping into the control of the masters of gravitation—the military. Both Kennedy and Khrushchev made desperate and only just successful attempts to keep the control of the situation in their own civilian hands and not let it fall into the hands of the military, the professionals of destruction. With one single accidentally or intentionally loosened atomic bomb the whole world would have gone up in flames. As a result of this situation we have today the partial nuclear test ban and the direct so-called hot line between Washington and Moscow, an almost desperate recognition of the threatening danger and the uncontrollable machinery of the State—a thin lifeline of our civilization.

The Cuban crisis was for Khrushchev and for Kennedy the limit situation in which they saw the abyss, the end of the world open under their feet. Perhaps it changed them from politicians to statesmen. In any case, it gave them the existential dread. When we later read their correspondence we learned that they were almost helpless—pilots of the ship of state which they had never learned to steer, engineers of a machinery of cosmic range the laws of which they did not understand. The present rulers of the state are in no better position. They are all in the position of Plato's captain. We are all ruled by the machinery of the state, servants of the mega-machine, instead of being its masters and ruling it.

THE MEGA-MACHINE OF DESTRUCTION

We shall now describe this machine.

During Hitler's war, there were thrown on Germany bombs with the explosive power of one million tons. In the total Hitler war, on all fronts, for seven years, five million tons of explosives were fired, out of rifles, guns, planes and tanks.

The United States today have in stock, ready to be shot and transported, and in preparation, bombs with an explosive power not of one or two Hitler wars, not of five or ten, of fifty or a hundred, not of five hundred or one thousand, not of two thousand or three thousand but of four thousand Hitler wars. Russia will soon match this capacity. Together, the United States and Russia have or will shortly have the explosive power of eight thousand Hitler wars. This explosive power grows every moment, it has been growing since you began reading. In Hitler's war, fifty-four million men, women, and children were killed. In order to annihilate the whole of humanity the explosive power of sixty Hitler wars would be sufficient. Instead of this, we have eight thousand Hitler wars in stock. The world can be destroyed today by the United States and Russia today some one hundred and sixty-seven times. According to the Pentagon, it takes four hundred megatons to wreck Russia. The

United States can thus annihilate Russia not once or twice, or twenty, but fifty times. Americans have an overkill capacity of 5,000 percent. And Russia can, or soon will be able to, destroy the United States often, with the same overkill capacity. Moreover, the nuclear weapon is only one of the three ABC weapons stockpiled by the state: atomic, bacteriological, and chemical. The so-called scientists of war do not speak any more of deaths and of losses in war, but of megadeaths, corpsemillions, or millioncorpses. A single Polaris submarine thus has the firepower of more than three Hitler wars. The United States alone has been building about fifty such ships, so that the entire Hitler war is represented by less than 1 percent of the American Polaris fleet, and the Polaris fleet is only a small part of the U.S. nuclear weapons arsenal. Yet its power is not big enough for the admirals; the new Poseidon missile will multiply the striking force of Polaris. At the same time, the Russians are building the same kind of ships with the same kind of bombs. Hitler in all his fiendishness had yet only a fraction of the destructive power that good men and earnest politicians, such as Kennedy, were in all seriousness and all good will prepared to shoot off in the name of freedom—as would Brezhnev and Kosygin, Johnson and Nixon. The partial nuclear test ban was only possible because it did not limit the production of these bombs.

Once exploded, these bombs destroy not only the country which they are directed at, but the whole world. In particular, like a boomerang, they destroy the country which shoots them off, because of the air currents in the Northern Hemisphere. Thus, if the United States would ever use its arsenal against Russia, Russia would not have to retaliate in order to destroy the United States. The air currents would do the job. The same goes for Russia. Thus, if war is the pursuit of national goals by force it is obvious that we cannot speak anymore of war. National goals cannot be pursued by nuclear weapons. Rather we are involved in the preparation of a suicide, indeed a murder orgy; for innocent and uninvolved countries would be destroyed, such as Canada, Iran, Sweden, Mexico. In the words of Dr. Sandoval Vallarta, the head of the Mexican Atomic Energy Commission: "Mr. McNamara is very optimistic. He says that in an atomic war nine out of ten Americans will die. No, ten out of ten will die—and six out of ten Mexicans." At a simulated atomic attack on the United States ten years ago, on October 17, 1958, with only 1,500 megatons—and Russia has already ten times that much nuclear power stockpiled—at such a small simulated attack the winds over Mexico were so full of radioactive fallout, of 600, 400 and 200 roentgen Strontium 90, each of these doses fatal for the population, and covered the country so completely that only a minority would have survived. There is actually no salvation in the case of such a war for any country in the Northern hemisphere. We would all die together. At this small attack died, according to the calculations, 90 percent of the American people. A nuclear attack, let alone an exchange of medium intensity today, would kill more than nine tenths of all people in the Northern Hemisphere, communists and capitalists without distinction.

Such a mass destruction of humanity, of course, cannot be called any more by the name of war. War up to now has been a well-defined act between the military forces of two nations the aim of which was to destroy the military forces of the enemy. Hitler's was the first war where large parts of the civil population were destroyed, the first genocidal war. In an atomic war not only the civilian population of the war-making powers but also those of the non-warring would be destroyed. Such a war then would not anymore be a war between two nations but a crime against humanity. It is therefore nonsensical to speak of nuclear war. There is only nuclear world destruction. The notion of war is not usable anymore. There is a sickness of rats where a tooth grows through the palate into the nose, through the nose into the eye, through the eye into the brain, killing the animal. Its gigantic growth destroys its purpose. So it is with the war weapons of today. Their gigantic growth has destroyed their purpose. It is nonsensical today to speak of defense in connection with nuclear weapons. We can only speak of destruction. When, for example, we say that Berlin, Korea or California would be defended with nuclear weapons what we actually say is that they would be destroyed by nuclear weapons; for after such a "defense" what we want to defend would not exist anymore—as we saw even in Vietnam where nuclear weapons have not been used. One hundred megaton bomb over Germany, one over France, and one over Britain, strategically placed, would destroy the whole of Europe. It is nonsense for NATO to speak of the nuclear defense of Europe. It can only destroy it. When Confucius was asked how he thought to create order and morality in the state his answer was: "By correcting names," meaning by calling each thing by its correct name. This is the same that Plato meant when he gave the prescription that everyone should do and think his own. To every situation we must give the corresponding concept, what is called defense today is destruction. Whenever we hear or read the word "defense" we should put instead the word "destruction." And whenever we hear or read the word 'war" we should put instead "the end of the world." Then we would see that we do not speak anymore of the defense of freedom but of its destruction, not of war but of the end of the world. The war ministries are ministries of the end of the world, the defense ministries are, in particular, self-destruction ministries. A nuclear policy for a big country such as the United States and Russia is suicide; for a small country such as France or Germany, who are hardly larger than Nevada or Wisconsin, it is a folly which is bigger even than Hitler's. At the aerial attacks on Dresden and Hamburg there arose fire storms which sucked the air out of the air raid shelters, tore the children from the hands of their parents into the fire, and seared the lungs of those who believed they had escaped the flames. In these firestorms died in Dresden 300,000 men, women and children; in Hamburg, 80,000. These firestorms were the results of attacks with 1,500 tons of TNT, that is of attacks which had 1/13th the power of Hiroshima and one thousandths of one percent the power of a hundred-megaton bomb. The firestorm which would be caused by a hundred-megaton bomb has a diameter of one hundred miles. Two such bombs, exploded over Philadelphia, would burn out, like a blowtorch, Philadelphia, New York, Harrisburg, Baltimore, and Washington; and would make the ocean boil 50 miles out. Two such bombs would be sufficient to burn out, like a blowtorch, the state of Tennessee. The Pentagon calls such destruction of all life and civilization "considerable thermal damage (fire)" and in the Kremlin they have similar euphemisms. They serve to build these figments of hell into the system of power politics—and to dim the minds of the nuclear citizens. The fiendish evil of an atomic war is either not being recognized or passed over in silence or trivialized. Thus, for example, Mr. A.F. Shinn, radiation ecologist of the Civil Defense Research Project's Agriculture team, whose work began in 1965, said in Oak Ridge on February 3, 1968, after two years of intensive study that "freshwater fish may be one answer to a sufficient protein diet for the U.S. population following a nuclear attack, research indicates. Although no prolonged shortage of raw or processed food stuffs are likely in such an emergency, temporary deficits will occur in some areas." He only forgot to mention two details: (1) that the freshwater fish will be radioactive and (2) that there will be no people left to enjoy it.

Another so-called expert on nuclear war, Hermann Kahn, says in his book, *On Thermonuclear War*, in discussing the genetic dangers of fall-out, that it is not so important if a few thousand children in future generations would be born with withered limbs if in this way we can maintain America's supremacy in Europe!

THE FALLACY OF SOVEREIGNTY: THE REASON OF STATE

Obviously, we have here a very special kind of mind and of morality. It is the so-called *raison d'etat,* the reason of state, which is diametrically opposed to common sense judgment and human morality. The reason of state is the morality of those who put the state above people; human morality is the morality of those who put people above the state. Jefferson once said there is never used so much wrong arithmetic as in the justification of war. This is especially true today. Thus, an atomic physicist, Edward Teller, in his book *The Legacy of Hiroshima*, makes in all seriousness the following so-called calculation: The total national wealth of the United States is fifteen hundred billion dollars. The United States can produce 500 billion dollars' worth of goods a year. Therefore, if it should be wiped out in an atomic war the survivors could in three to five years restore what has been lost. Teller does not see the development of thousands of years which led to the tremendous productive apparatus of 500 billion, now 800 billion a year, nor can he imagine the miserable plight of the survivors, if any, who, as President Truman said, would envy the dead. He believes quite simply that these crazed and wandering hordes could keep up the production of the vanished United States. Another atomic physicist, Ralph A. Lapp, in his book *Kill and Overkill*, says one can only admire the elegant simplicity of Teller's arithmetic. According to Teller's argument, the old Greeks, with what they knew and just a few essential instruments, would have been able within five years to jump into the 20th century.

What is amazing is that thinking such as Teller's is being printed, read, and believed. Such thinking is an example of what Ortega y Gasset calls the thinking of the "specialized barbarian." In the *Revolt of the Masses* Ortega says that scientists and politicians live in our civilization as unconcerned as savages in the primeval forest. Like them, they take everything around them for granted. They do not stop to realize that it was the thought and sweat of millions of people through hundreds of generations that created today's civilization. These scientists and politicians live, he says, without the sense of time, like savages—and, we may add, like criminals. The criminal has no sense of time. What others have achieved in the long and hard labor of a lifetime they believe they can seize in a short and violent act and hold with the same justification. They have no respect for the past and no concept of the future. To build up, says Ortega, one needs the sense of time, the feeling of what he calls the Project, the plan to be worked out in a lifetime. The good takes time, the bad can be done in a moment. To create a life takes nine months and many years of growth and education, to snuff it out takes a second.

What is true for the life of the individual is also true for the life of collective bodies. He who does not have the sense of time believes that civilization grows by itself like the primeval forest. In Chapter 10 of his book, entitled "Primitivism and History", Ortega says that those who enjoy the blessings of civilization without bothering to maintain civilization will at the flick of a hand be left without civilization. The modern barbarian believes that the civilization into which he was born is as spontaneous and self-producing as is nature, "and ipso facto he is changed into primitive man." For him, civilization is the forest. The basic values of culture are of no interest to him and he has no contact with them. Hence the disproportion between the complex subtlety of the problems and the coarseness of the minds that should study them. It is painful, says Ortega, to hear relatively cultured people discuss the most elementary problems of the day. They seem like rough farmhands trying with thick, clumsy fingers to pick up a needle lying on the table. Political and social subjects are handled with the same crude instruments of thought which served two hundred years ago to tackle situations two hundred times less complex. In Chapter 12, "The Barbarism of 'Specialization'" he speaks of the so-called intellectuals, educated professionals who believe because they understood one subject, they understand all. Today's scientist, says Ortega, is the prototype of the mass-man. The scientific man, because he has to reduce the sphere of his interest, loses progressively contact with other branches of science and thus the integral interpretation of the universe which alone deserves the name of science.

As specialist, the scientist becomes the modern barbarian, a knowledgeable ignoramus who hides behind his specialty. Knowing well his own tiny corner of the universe and being radically ignorant of the rest, he is particularly dangerous today because he can use the State itself for his barbaric ends. The State, says Ortega, has in our time become a tremendously powerful machine which, due to the quantity and precision of its means, works with marvelous efficiency. The mass man will be inclined more and more to use this machine for his own ends. The State is soulless as is he himself, and thus he is convinced that he is the State; and he confuses the State with society. He will more and more tend to set its machinery in motion, on whatsoever pretext, to crush beneath it any creative minority that disturbs him—politically, ideologically, or economically. Since, however, the state is in the last instance only a machine the maintenance of which depends on precisely these creative powers of society, the state itself, by misusing and sucking the marrow out of society, will die the rusty death of a machine, a death, says Ortega, which is more cadaverous than that of a living organism. The State will become one gigantic junkpile.

All this, says Ortega y Gasset, has happened before. It was the pitiable fate of antiquity. "Already at the time of the Antonines (2nd Century), the state overwhelms society with its anti-vital supremacy. Society begins to be enslaved, to be unable to live except in the service of the state. The whole of life is bureaucratized. What results? The bureaucratization of life brings about the absolute decay in all orders. Wealth diminishes, births are few. Then the State, in order to attend to its own needs, forces on still more the bureaucratization of human existence. This bureaucratization to the second power is the militarization of society. The State's most urgent need is its apparatus of war, its army. First of all, the State is the producer of security (that security, be it remembered, of which the mass-man is born). Hence, above all, an army. The Severi, of African origin, militarize the world. Vain task! Misery increases. Women are every day less fruitful, even soldiers are lacking. After the time of the Severi, the army has to be recruited from foreigners.

> Is the paradoxical, tragic process of Statism now understood? Society, that it may live better, creates the State as

an instrument. Then the State gets the upper hand and society has to begin to live for the State.... This is what State intervention leads to: The people are converted into fuel to feed the mere machine which is the State. The skeleton eats up the flesh around it. The scaffolding becomes the owner and tenant of the house. [Ortega]

What happened in Rome and brought about the fall of the Roman Empire that, says Ortega, is also the greatest danger for human society today: the State itself. The title of Chapter 13 is "The Greatest Danger: The State." The greatest danger that threatens society—and this was written forty years ago, before World War II—the greatest danger that threatens civilization today is the State. It meddles with everything, absorbs all spontaneous social life, especially in the militarized countries, where opposition to the State's often ill-advised and ruinous adventures is called treason. Ortega's analysis was clairvoyant. Today, in Russia and in the United States, one sees exactly the same development as in Rome. The apparatus of the State draws into itself the life of society and its vital resources. What was means becomes end. The State, founded in order to enhance the life of society, sucks the forces of society into itself to expand its own existence. Bureaucracy becomes its own end. The military apparatus grows only in order to grow, like the rat's "tooth." Such transposition of means and end is in ethics called metentalosis, the means becoming ends. In the United States and in Russia the military apparatus devours the society which it is supposed to defend.

Both the Western and Eastern nations today use the largest percentage of their internal capital formation for military purposes. In Mexico, a sane country, this percentage is five percent. In the United States it is 60 percent, in Great Britain, 42 percent, in France 35 percent, in the Soviet Union 34 percent, and in the respective allied countries, Greece, Czechoslovakia, Poland, East Germany, etc. between 30 and 16 percent. Both the Eastern and the western world today are warfare states. The military budgets of the five nuclear nations are as big as the total gross national product of all the world's developing nations together. All this can only lead, as it was in the case in Rome, to bankruptcy or to war, or both. As in Rome, we see how the value of money declines, the balance of payments worsens, hidden unemployment increases for in spite of unheard-of production the largest part of it is unproductive and consists of arms. The civilian society stagnates, schools, hospitals, roads, housing, all that makes the life of the individual materially worthwhile, is jacked up by the behemoth of war—and more and more it sucks up the life itself of the individual. At the same time, the production of weapons increases, by up to 40 percent a year. The Secretary of Defense (that is, of Destruction) of the United States said on August 13, 1963, before a Senate committee, in order to justify the partial nuclear test ban, that production of nuclear bombs in the last two years had risen by one hundred percent. What did this mean? It meant that two years before the United States could destroy Russia only 12 times and that then it could do so 24 times. It meant that in 1961 the United States had stockpiled only 1,000 Hitler wars and in 1963, 2,000. In the same way the Soviet Union doubled its intercontinental ballistic missile force in 1966. In 1967 it could destroy the United States 20 times while it could do so only 10 times at the beginning of 1966.

This mad logic is the logic of the reason of state. It is a logic of irrationality, that is, of rationalization. Those who are caught in it have their own jargon. They speak of survivability and vitality, but not of people but of bombs. Our hardened nuclear missile sites have survivability and vitality, that is, they are capable of surviving us. When we are all dead our desolate land will be capable of spitting out bombs against Russia, and we would have the consolation of dying in the knowledge that the others will too.

The whole nuclear so-called politics rests on a fundamental contradiction. We trust that the enemy will be deterred by our weapons from making war. But this can only be the case if he is rational. And if he is rational he can be persuaded; we don't need weapons; we can make treaties with him. Again, even if he is rational, he may not be deterred, as Russia could not deter Kennedy in 1962 (even though the Cuban missiles were no closer to us than the Turkish missiles were to Russia). The reason of State itself is irrational, so that no rational argument holds within it. Nuclear power cannot be "balanced," just as the balance of power has failed throughout history, most recently in 1914 and 1939. If ever a madman came to power in a nuclear nation, such as Hitler, he would only have to push a button in order to have his boldest dreams of chaos surpassed by mad reality. The situation, far from being of deterrence, is, on the contrary, an irresistible invitation for madmen—for the crew of Plato's ship of State.

The whole history of so-called power politics rests on a logical fallacy and its course has been correspondingly disastrous.

THE HISTORY OF SOVEREIGNTY: THE FEUDAL ESSENCE OF THE MODERN STATE

How is it possible that modern nations such as the United States with its liberal revolution of 1776, or Russia with its proletarian revolution of 1917 can make the same mistakes as ancient Rome with its soldier emperors?

The reason is that today's state is only quantitatively different from Rome. It reaches macrocosmically out to the planets and microcosmically down into our genes. But qualitatively, morally, there is no difference between our state and Rome. The same morality rules in our state as it did in Rome, the reason of state. The state sets its own supremacy, its "sovereignty", above morality. A good man like Truman can give the order to drop the atomic bomb, abetted by a good man such as Arthur Compton; a good man such as Khrushchev gave the order to explode a hundred-million ton bomb; and a good man such as Kennedy could have given the order for atomic war in the Cuban crisis. They did it not as individuals but as rulers of the State. They believe that the morality of the state is different from that of the individual. This was exactly the error Plato wanted to correct; and the same that Pope John XXIII in his Encyclical *Pacem in Terris* called the root of all our disorders.

Machiavelli shows that the reason of state of his contemporary princes is the same as that of the Roman Emperors. We can show that the morality of our gigantic states is the same as that of the Renaissance princes. A direct line leads from the tragedy of Rome to the tragedy that threatens us. One may say without exaggeration that nuclear war if it should come is the direct consequence of Roman militarism—a militarism which we repeat, and which came down to us through a causal chain which leads inexorably from Rome to our own days. Because of Rome's militarism the Germans conquered Rome; for this militarism did not strengthen but weakened Rome, sucking dry the vital sources of Roman society. The fall of Rome resulted in political and economic anarchy. Money lost its value; the only value left was that of land. The central government disappeared, the empire disintegrated into uncountable small regions each of which needed a strong military organization as protection against foreign and domestic bandits. These organizations were created by using the value of the land. The free men of the region put themselves under the protection of the strongest offering him their military help in exchange for land as payment. If they were landowners themselves they offered him their land for protection and got it back in fee as payment for their services. These land tenures together with the military obligation inhering in them were called 'beneficia" and later fiefs and feuds. Thus the feudal system arose. The feudal contract was a mutual obligation for protection on the one hand and feudal tenure on the other. Every feudal relationship developed according to the temperament of the feudal lord and his success, and either increased or diminished. Out of some of these feudal tenures arose our national states of today: out of the Grand Duchy of Normandy, England; out of the Grand Duchy of Kiev, Russia; out of the Isle de France, France; out of the Mark of Brandenburg, Germany. As the feudal system followed the decline of Rome, so absolutism followed the decline of the feudal system. Just as the feudal system was the consequence of that Roman tragedy so the Absolute State was the consequence of the tragedy of the feudal system. The tragedy of Rome was the exploitation of the civil society by the military state; and the tragedy of the feudal system was exactly the same exploitation. Again, the military state exploited the civil society and again both perished together.

The feudal contract had its justification as long as anarchy and chaos stalked the land. As soon, however, as chaos subsided, regular communications arose between the various regions and the civil society was resurrected, reborn in commerce and industry, around 900 A.D., the protection of the feudal lord became unnecessary; the peasants and the citizens of the new cities instituted their own communities, administration and police. The feudal lord became unemployed. But since he had not learned anything but to fight and did not want to sit idly in his castle, he provoked private fights on his own. The baron became the robber baron. Instead of protecting his men he exploited them, forced them into military service, or sold them as soldiers to foreign princes. The protector became the oppressor, the defender the attacker. Ever new wars were artificially produced, and the victors advanced from feudal lords, subject to feudal contract, to supreme masters, above the feudal or any other law, to sovereigns. The increasing prosperity of the region, the labor of peasants and workers, merchants and bankers, flowed through a thousand perversions of the old feudal contract into the coffers of the sovereign. He administered his land as a fief which first he pretended to have received from the Emperor and then directly from the Lord, ruling "by the grace of God." His wealth forced him to develop a fiscal bureaucracy, and his army a military bureaucracy. Thus arose absolute monarchy. The absolute monarch was the head of a new military-fiscal bureaucracy. The culmination of this development was in France Louis XIV, in England Henry VIII and Elizabeth I, in Russia Peter the Great, in Germany the Great Elector and Frederick the Great. The whole nation was seen as the personal property of these rulers. They augmented their realm and were proud that their wars did as little damage as possible to their civil society. As Frederick the Great said to his generals when, on June 1st, 1740, he took over the reins of government: "Gentlemen, I want you to protect my country, not to ruin it." When, through the sovereigns' wars, these countries were ruined after all, as was France in the wars of Louis XIV, there followed the rational revolutions which, through the political time lag, came always too late. The revolution against Louis XIV was made against Louis XVI, the revolution against Henry VIII against Charles I, the revolution against Peter the Great against Nicholas II, and the revolution against Frederick the Great against William II.

At the time of these revolutions the dynasties had already ceased to be masters of the fiscal-military bureaucracies. These bureaucracies had become independent and could very well exist without the sovereign. They became, without any change, parts of the new republics. Therefore, the new organization of the state, the republic or democracy, changed nothing in the old reason of state. The old notion of sovereignty was taken over intact from the deposed absolute rulers by the new republics. The great revolutionaries took over the military-bureaucratic apparatus of the preceding regime and elaborated, refined, and enlarged it for the same ends as before. Napoleon took over and improved the military machine of the French Republic which in its turn had taken it over from the fallen monarch and tremendously developed it in the social invention of the levée en masse, universal military machine of the German Republic; indeed, he received it directly from the hands of its Field Marshall-President, von Hindenburg, just as the German Republic had taken it over from the emperor and the emperor from the King of Prussia, whose predecessors had built it up in 700 years of uninterrupted labor. Trotsky took over the military apparatus of the Czar because, as Lenin said at the time, "history makes the military problem the essence of the political problem," so that within three years the revolutionary Red Army contained 300,000 former Czarist officers. And even the American Revolution had in Lafayette and Steuben the connection between the forces of the young republic and the old European monarchies, against whose Machiavellian power politics it was explicitly founded and whose draft dodgers it welcomed by the hundreds of thousands throughout the 19th century.

Neither the German nor the Russian nor the American nor the French nor the English, the Indian, the Chinese or any other revolution has done away with the sovereignty of the State, its power over life and death of its citizens. No revolution has, until this day, separated the civil society from the military state. Revolutions, up to now, have not meant anything but the transition of the sovereign power from the proprietor, the absolute monarch, to the administrators, the Republican officials—and these were often more efficient and competent sovereigns than the old monarchs. Louis XIV was a dilettante compared to Napoleon, Nicholas II a buffoon compared to Trotsky, William II a midget compared to Hitler, George III a small-time operator compared to Churchill, Roosevelt and General Marshall who really knew how to make war.

Today's national state is the culmination of this whole development, this trilogy of tragedies. The tragedy of Rome was military despotism, the tragedy of feudalism was military absolutism, the tragedy of today's democracy is military gigantism. All three tragedies have the same reason, the exploitation of the civil society by the military state. Today's national state is nothing but a monstrously inflated feudal state, a fief entrusted, supposedly by God, to the politicians who run it. Today's generals think in terms of the old tournaments and play war games with their electronic computers. The results compound the fallacy of sovereignty by fallacies of strategy. There are many examples to choose from, such as the generals' predictions of the end of the Vietnamese War or the development of the F-111. The following are two especially absurd and macabre results. The Pentagon recently discovered that its anti-missile system, bases on the anti-missile missile Sprint, would incinerate the United States, because exploding the missiles against which the anti-missile missile is to "defend" the country, at between 5,000 and 50,000 feet altitude, the exploding missile would incinerate the land, and thus the defense against it would bring about what the attack was aimed at. "At 5,000 feet," said Secretary Robert S. McNamara of February 3, 1968, "destruction would be total over about 150 square miles" for each 10-megaton missile intercepted by our Defense, that is, our Destruction. "A low-level detonation also would mean that the fireball of the explosion would touch the ground and that tons of earth would be sucked into the atmosphere. This could occur from altitudes of 10,000 feet or more and would cause windblown radioactive fallout in lethal quantities hundreds of miles away." This, of course, the military did not tell the country when they asked for the billions to develop Sprint. Therefore, and this was called "new information released by the Pentagon," much more reliance is now being placed on the long-range Spartan missile, effective in space, which would destroy incoming missiles "at altitudes of perhaps 100 miles. Unofficial reports were that the Administration plans to deploy around 1,000 Spartans and only 100-200 of the Sprints at the 15-20 antimissile sites in the 'thin' system under construction." That is to say, there will be 50 Spartans deployed around each of the 20 missile sites. Suppose they explode only half their number, 25 ten-megaton bombs or five billion tons of explosive, that is, half a million Hiroshimas or 1,000 total Hitler wars—with enough havoc over the Northern Hemisphere to wipe out all life. This is the effect if the 'thin' 5-billion-dollar antiballistic defense system now under construction works. Again, the military do not tell us this. As is seen, this is computerized quackery playing with our unborn children's and grandchildren's life.

The second example is the so-called no-city strategy. This is a particularly ingenious gimmick of the computerized quacks—G. Wright Mills called them "crackpot realists"—who operate on the body politic. This "new strategy" changed the data of nuclear war being fed into the computers. So far, the war games had always given as result the end of the American nation. This was changed by programming to so-called no-city strategy according to which neither Americans nor Russians will zero in on cities but only on military installations. In this way the computer cut the losses of the United States from 180 million to 80 million, which left a hundred million survivors for the next war. The only drawback of the new strategy was that the Russians announced they wouldn't play the game but would zero in on cities. Senator Russell, in a speech on April 11, 1962, said it was nonsense to feed the honor code of medieval knights into electronic computers—yet this strategy is one of the official strategies of the nuclear Don Quixotes in the Pentagon.

As Don Quixote's, so their unreal play will break down in reality if war should come. There will happen the same as at the end of Rome and of the Middle Ages: our State will go down not in spite but because of our immense armaments. What was thought to be protection will be destruction. History, as it always has, will again demonstrate the fallacy of sovereignty.

Just as Rome broke down under its crushing armaments, so that the empire was but an empty shell crumbling at the first strike of the barbarians, so it was at the end of the Middle Ages. The immense armaments broke down the State. On October 24, 1415, 50,000 heavily armored French knights faced 13,000 English archers on the field of Agincourt. It had been raining all night and, in order not to sink into the morass, the heavily armored knights remained all night sitting on their horses in the plowed fields. When day broke they had to get down from their horses, onto which they had been lifted by cranes, into the slimy ooze, into which they sank deeper and deeper. When the battle began at 11 o'clock in the morning they were unable to move and could only stand there waiting for the blow to strike. The English began the attack, hammering the plain of armor like a gigantic anvil. It was slaughter, and at four in the afternoon all was over.

What was true at Agincourt is a million times true today. The tremendously armed Americans and the tremendously armed Russians stood opposite each other on October 24, 1962, helpless, waiting for the missiles to fly. Both civilians and military of these nations, and with them of all the world, are helpless objects of potential slaughter. If nuclear war should come we all would be drawn into the morass by the weight of our monstrous armaments as were the knights of Agincourt. On the other hand, we cannot wage conventional war either, for compared with the billion men of the Communist nations we are a very small nation of only 200 million and can be bled white by a tenth-rate country such as Vietnam. This means that the age of military power is at an end.

Insofar as we still think nationally, we think feudal terms in a nuclear context. We must liberate our thinking from these old grooves and direct it into new channels. We must break with history.

THE REVOLUTION AGAINST WAR

In the Preamble to the Constitution of UNESCO, the United Nations Educational Scientific and Cultural Organization, we read the famous words: "Since wars begin in the minds of men, it is in the minds of men that the defenses of peace must be constructed." Pope John XXIII says in *Pacem in Terris* that braking the armament race and eliminating it is impossible unless disarmament is so complete and efficient that it includes the minds of men. Every single person, says the Pope, must in his own heart stamp out the fear and nightmare of war. This, he says, is only possible if it is understood that true and secure peace between nations does not consist in a balance of terror but in mutual trust. In other words, the battlefield of peace is in the heart of man. When the United States was founded, it relied on its distance from power politics in the Atlantic Ocean. Today, this distance has shrunk. The distance from power politics must now be found in the heart of each of us. Peace now is a matter of morality and not of weaponry. Politics itself must be overcome. The sovereign national state is obsolete both in concept and in reality.

Its power consists exclusively in the obedience of its own citizens. As soon as the citizens understand completely the suicidal game that is being played with them they will simply refuse to play. At that moment the military state will break down and the civil society, human life itself, will become sovereign. Existence itself will come into its own. As Jacques Maritain says, in his book *Man and the State*, every citizen of a warlike nation state is a vassal of this state. He must liberate himself from it and not lend it the force of his own life. The sovereign state is a fetish which puts the state in the place of God—the same lethal blasphemy committed by the Roman Emperors, and particularly by Constantine, who put himself at the head of the church—a lure and a trap from which Christianity has never recovered. The reason of the state must be replaced by moral reason, the immorality of the state by the morality of the human person. We must put ourselves consciously above the military state and make the state our servant, not our master. We must think in civilian, not in military terms. Thus, instead of spending 30 billion dollars a year for the destruction of the South Vietnamese we could spend this amount for their instruction and production. This would give $2,000 to every man, woman and child, or $8,000 per family per year, in a country where the average annual income is $113. We could make them all rich—and rich people don't go communist. But such creative solutions are beyond the military mind that rules us, indeed, beyond our own military-mindedness. We would never give $30 billion to a tiny country like South Vietnam. It just isn't worth it. But it is worth it if we can use the money to destroy it. Then, suddenly, South Vietnam is a most important country.

In a word, we love war better than peace.

There are two reasons for this, one of cognition and one of will. The first is that we do not really know what peace is. We know what war is because natural science today is largely the science of war. We know how to wage war, but we do not know how to wage peace. There is no science of peace. The reason is that the philosophers of the Renaissance and the Enlightenment developed only natural but not moral philosophy into science. Yet, their true purpose was moral knowledge. Before the minds of the philosophical interpreters of natural science and its mathematical foundations, Descartes and Leibniz, there stood with great clarity the vision of a Science of Value, or as it was then called, a Moral Science, to be established by the side of natural science and based, like it, on the *mathesis universalis*, which today is called logic. Descartes' goal was not only to reformulate a natural science, but also a "mathematical morality: that was the bold program. Nothing in the development and the system of Descartes can be rightly understood unless this is understood" (Borkenau). For Leibniz the differential calculus was only part of a large calculus of universal logic applicable to all the sciences and humanities, so that "two philosophers who disagreed about a particular point, instead of arguing fruitlessly, would take out their pencils and calculate." As for Descartes and Leibniz, so for the other philosophers of that great age: the science of morality presented itself based on the methods of natural science. Spinoza applied the geometrical method to the whole of ethics, Locke wrote his *Essay* as prolegomena to "a subject very remote from this," namely morality and revealed religion, and showed "that moral knowledge is as capable of real certainty as mathematics." The full title of Hume's Treatise is *A Treatise on Human Nature: Being an Attempt to Introduce the Experimental Method of Reasoning into Moral Subjects*. And even Berkeley used epistemology only as a tool for theological ethics, the rules of which "have the same immutable universal truth with propositions of geometry."

What made the natural philosophers soar ahead and the moral philosophers stagnate was that the former did, and the latter did not understand the Newtonian method. This was the paradox of the Newtonian achievement. Natural philosophy became science, moral philosophy, in spite of all the attempts of Renaissance and enlightenment, and even of Newton himself, has remained philosophy and degenerated into ideology. As a result, while the natural philosophers brought about the scientific revolution the moral philosophers only brought about political revolutions. And while the scientific revolution changed the earth, the political revolutions changed fundamentally nothing. The great evil of absolutism, the sovereignty of the State above the moral law, is today stronger than ever. As a result, we have the combination of natural science with the amoral sovereign state.

The first task of the revolution against war is an intellectual one. We must bring about the moral science our predecessors intended but failed to achieve. At the end of his *Optics*, Newton says, after describing the method of analysis and synthesis: "And if natural philosophy in all its parts by pursuing this method shall at length be perfected the bounds of moral philosophy will also be enlarged." Unfortunately, Newton himself, in his studies in morality and religion, which took many more years of his life than his studies in nature, did not use this method; instead of applying number to observation he applied it to speculation, instead of mathematical he made numerological studies. Some philosophers have discussed what the Newtonian method would mean when applied to morals. Yet nobody has so far realized this program though it is relatively easy to state: to apply the Newtonian method of analysis and synthesis to social and moral phenomena means to break down these phenomena into their primary qualities and reconstruct the latter in a coherent formal system. Primary qualities of society and man, as Susanne Langer has stated long ago, will resemble the obvious properties of man and society as little as the obvious properties of things resemble protons and electrons. We have to get away, thus, from the obvious properties of social and moral phenomena, as Galileo got away from the obvious properties of things in motion. Much of our present-day psychology, sociology, philosophy and political so-called science will then turn out to be ideology, just as the Aristotelian-Aquinian dogma of Galileo's time turned out to be ideology—through construction, that is, without counterparts in reality.

What we have to do, thus, is to bring about the complement of Renaissance and Enlightenment: we must apply the Newtonian method to human values. The results will be a moral science by the side of natural science—a science of peace by the side of the science of war. Thus we would bring about the union of cosmic consciousness and moral insight which is the intellectual task of our age.

How can this be done? Ethics, which today is still as archaic as was Aristotelian physics, must leap forward not only to the modern age but beyond it to the age of planetary humanity. Moral philosophers, not yet able even to define the nature of goodness or to influence, let alone guide, human fellowship on earth, must produce the tools of planetary ethics. Yet, we are not entirely unprepared. Philosophers, from Plato to Whitehead, have charted the course, projecting to join mathematics with the good; George E. Moore has approached the definition of the primary properties of value; and Bergson, in *The Two Sources of Morality and Religion*, has worked out the cosmic program. What is left to do is to pull the strands together and create a science of ethics as precise and universal as the science of nature. Even this task is well on the way. We can already see what these philosophers divined: that the science of ethics has indeed its exact laws, that they can be formulated with precision, and applied to social and moral phenomena. It is not utopian then, to believe that a science of morality is possible—indeed, if we did not we would have to hold that all philosophers from Plato onward had been mistaken and that a few modern sophists are right. Once we believe, however, that a science of ethics is possible, we are obliged to work for its realization. The future of peace will see Institutes of Value Research on many a campus—institutes which will have the exact function that Plato outlined for his research institute, the Nocturnal Council, in *The Laws* (967 E): "To grasp the laws which control the stars and to apply them harmoniously to the institutions and rules of ethics"—to combine, that is, cosmic order with human morality and to find the logic that rules the universe without and within us. This logic will be a new specialty: that of axiologic or value logic, which will structure and suffuse all humanistic and social subject matter, as today mathematics structures and suffuses all natural science subject matter.

Once this science is on the way the same will happen as happened in the development of nature science, a refinement and deepening of human sensitivity. Natural science refined and deepened our understanding of the problems of nature to the very limits of the sensitivity of our measuring instruments—down to the quantum and up to the nuclear. Moral science ought to deepen and refine our understanding of moral nature, to the very limits of our own sensitivity, down to the suffering of an ant and up to the agonies of war. In this way the fulfillment of our intellectual task will make possible that of method, to technology, in particular that of war, so moral science should lead, through its inherent method, to the techniques of goodness, in particular those of peace.

Clarity of moral purpose, thus, would lead to decisiveness of moral action, and the moral revolution lead necessarily to the existential revolution. As the scientific revolution of the Renaissance and the Enlightenment was accompanied by an exhilarating rise of extensive vitality, an explosion of the will to act, so the moral revolution of the future ought to be accompanied by a similar rise of intensive vitality, an explosion of the will to live. This awareness of Life, and the circumstances of life, ought to be occupied with an awareness of Death and the circumstances of death. It will then be possible clearly to distinguish between the two kinds of state and society, the natural of life and the artificial of death: the family of man and the military state. We have discussed the latter; we must now examine the former.

The natural society of man, to which belongs the civil function of the state, is based on the laws of the universe itself; the earth's circling around the sun, the currents of air and water, sun and rain, the sequence of day and night, the rhythm of the seasons, the whole balance of nature that makes possible our existence. Each of us is the offspring of a long chain of generations, created in billions of years out of primal matter, each of us a progeny of the universe, in the sense of Walt Whitman:

> Immense have been the preparations for me,
> Faithful and friendly the arms that have help'd me.
> Cycles ferried my cradle, rowing and rowing like cheerful
> boatmen,
> For room to me stars kept aside in their own rings,
> They sent influences to look after what was to hold me.
> My embryo has never been torpid, nothing could overlay
> it.

For it the nebula cohered into an orb,
The long slow strata piled to rest it on,
Vast vegetables gave it sustenance,
Monstrous sauroids transported it in their mouths and
deposited it with care.
All forces have been steadily employ'd to complete and
delight me,
Now on this spot I stand with my robust soul.

In this soul I know what is right and what is wrong. I know that all men are brothers with me on this planet.

This natural society is so obvious as never to become visible; it is a truth in the depth of our spirit. But is overlaid by the slogans and divisions of history. The split between the two societies is a split within us. With our minds we are in the fragmented society of a national state, with our soul we live in the oneness of humanity. Each of us is victim, or potential victim of the one, and harbinger of the other. In all of us is the transposition between men and what used to be the citizen but is rapidly becoming the subject. This transposition is found strikingly, even amusingly, illustrated in the book *Five Journeys from Jakarta* by Maslyn Williams, a book on a new nation still smarting from the indignities of the old colonialism. Williams attended a meeting where a lovely young girl made the predictable speech: "Crush Malaysia and free our neighbors from British imperialism" and all that. He was incensed at the "worn out phrases… would kiss her and stop the flow of words, words… give her a baby, make her mother, turn her back into a pretty girl instead of a robot with a tape recorder for a brain." But a moment later the mask fell, and the girl was revealed. Her brothers were making plans for a feast day dance. "I wondered why they should die in Malaysia, and who will gain," she says. "She stopped," Williams notes, "and looked down as if she had run out of words, and there was quiet."

All over the world people feel the moral antagonism between system and life that splits mankind into states, and man himself into allegiances. There is a new sensitivity abroad, found in various degrees not only in individuals but in large groups of society. We could mention the desegregation revolution which is an awakening to human dignity and expectation on a large scale. We could mention the new and, it seems, definitive awareness of the clergy, of their own independent moral role against the immorality of the State, returning to the pre-Constantinian awareness of the early church, after centuries of subservience to the State. In the words of Dr. Eugene Blake, the new secretary of the National Council of the Churches of Christ: "In World War II we were asked to regard as the ultimate fiends of humanity the Germans and the Japanese against whom we fought by the side of our great and good friends, the Russians and Chinese. Today we are asked to regard these same Russians and Chinese as the ultimate fiends and accept the former fiends as our great and good friends. We may be stupid, but not that stupid." In this confusion, he says, there is only one truth, that of Jesus Christ: "Love your enemies, do good to those that hate you." Christianity, says Dr. Blake, is radical, though Christians are often docile and conservative. The same could be said of science and the scientists, and of education and the educators. Their work is the future, but many live in the past. Yet, it is the educators who will be put to the test. For, important though the two groups mentioned are, more important is a third group awakening today to moral awareness, the group of those who carry the future and will be filling colleges and universities in the years to come, today's youth. They see—and this is a peculiar phenomenon common to the young people all over the world, but especially to those in the two great nuclear nations, the United States and Russia—that the old forms of thought and society are outmoded because they are immoral. These rebels have grown in the last ten years in both countries, from about one percent to about five percent of all youth. If the trend continues they will, in another ten years, grow to 25 percent. Although this awakening sometimes takes peculiar forms one should not be misled by outer appearances. There is a serious and profound core in this sudden rally of the young.

These young people are not political, they are moral revolutionaries. And they are not really revolutionaries for they are re-discovering some very old truths. They are only trying to bring society up to date, to adequate it to its own professional moral standards. They are discovering the inalienable moral truth within, and of, their own selves. This awakening is called the new left in the United States and may be called the same in Russia. Both movements go back to the original inspiration that formed their states and are opposed to its later perversions. Their spokesmen are Paul Goodman here and Yevgeny Yevtushenko there. Both speak the same language. Paul Goodman, in the Life-Time Special Report, "The Young Americans", speaks of "moral youth in an immoral society" and describes their contempt for the society they live in, the hypocrisy and immorality of what they call the "Liberal establishment," and of the schools they call its "factories." Yevtushenko speaks in the same terms of the Communist Establishment, especially in his *Precocious Autobiography*, and his poems whose readings draw 15,000 persons and are the Russian equivalent to American demonstrations. This unrest, say both Paul Goodman and Yevtushenko, is not an ordinary generational rebellion, it is the "existential" politics, unideological and hence really neither left nor right, the moral revolt that happens when a dominant system of society has come to seem senile and absurd. It seeks existential truth, Pravda. The Russian young men and women say, *mutatis mutandis*, the same that a high school girl, Sara Greenfelder, says in the Life-Time Report: "I'm sort of sick of the United States [of Russia]—not my immediate environment but the moral standards of most people. Adults in this country are always playing games. They can't do or say what they want. In public they're forced to be hypocrites by our system, which is all based on money" (on power, the Russian young people say). In both countries the young rebel against their elders' conformity; and it is this conformity the military state thrives on. Hence the rebellion is largely directed against this state. It is a true revolution against war—but against war as the symptom of a moral disease. In the words of David Harris, former student-body president of Stanford, who has refused induction: "No new politician is going to bring an end to what we object to in this country. What we need is a new way of life, a brotherhood of man."

Thus, there is already more to the new moral humanity than the call for the development of a new science to create it. There is the commitment of an increasing part of humanity to this new vision. Once it is joined to intellectual understanding, the methods of peace will unfold as elaborately and efficiently as those of war. This will bring about a change deeper than any that has ever taken place in history. It will lead to the emancipation of the individual person from the State, the emancipation of the civil society from the military apparatus. Peace has nothing to do with capitalism, communism or any other ism, any economic or ideological difference. The democratic as the totalitarian citizen dies for the same kind of fiction, of "sovereignty," as did his medieval ancestors. *"Ce sont toujours les mômes qui su font tuer"* (Maritain). The revolution against war is a rebellion of the morituri who have stopped to salute Caesar. The subjects of the military system have suddenly become conscious of their fetters. They want to live.

The rebellion of the young is nothing but the first rubbing of the explosion of the will to live which will sweep away the third rider of the Apocalypse.

To give this movement power, to lead it from utopia to science, philosophers must concentrate as thoroughly, and as ingeniously, on the essence of man as our predecessors—at the beginning of the modern age—concentrated on the essence of nature. The Renaissance was a new beginning, born from external and internal events, the exploration of the globe and the feeling of individual independence. The new epoch into which we are entering is born from external and internal exploration: we are the generation that has seen a man floating in outer space, above the terrestrial globe; and our youth is exploring, often desperately, the expanses of inner space. But the feeling of individual independence is now one of individual interdependence. We have seen this earth as one from above. We must now form it as one from within.

CHAPTER X
Book Proposal

EDITOR'S NOTE

According to Hartman's son, Jan, his father was at work on a book with the same name as the previous essay, The Revolution Against War, *when he died. In a letter to the Institute written in 1984, Jan mentions that he had helped his father with writing part of* The Revolution Against War.

During archival research in 2018, we discovered a book outline, in proposal form, that I believe is the text that Jan referred to. The proposal is entitled simply, "Outline." I conclude that, most likely, it is the outline of the book Hartman intended to entitle, "The Revolution Against War."

That proposal, in its outline form, is presented next. As you read it, you will recognize bits that later made their way into Hartman's autobiography, Freedom to Live, *and also to bits that allude to several essays in the current volume.*

Hartman died with this book unfinished, unpublished, and unread. Eerily, this is much the same state as the adoption— or, rather the lack of adoption by the United States and other world powers—of the revolution that Hartman argued so stridently for.

OUTLINE OF BOOK PROPOSAL

Peace has been sought for thousands of years in vain. The horror of nuclear bombs has been shown in dozens of books, but they have made no impression sufficient for humanity to abjure war. This shows that something more is needed today than description and exhortation.

Writing about it will not do anymore; one has to give himself heart, mind and soul to the task of making peace. And one has to do so full time.

I have dedicated the last thirty years to this cause, full time, and now I feel the moment has come to step forward and tell my story. Therefore the book is written as a personal narrative. It is an autobiography; and it is a mirror of the age. It so happens that each of the significant events of the past fifty years has had a significant counterpart in my life. Thus, each chapter of the book opens with an episode of my life, an episode which is connected with, and symbolic for, the content of the chapter in question. This not only makes the presentation authentic, but it is designed to give the reader, at the end, the feeling that he knows his situation in the world, and that he is ready to act.

This book has a Dedication:

> To You, the Reader,
> Who Will Decide
> My Life or My Death.

The chapters are introduced by a Prologue and an Introduction.

THE PROLOGUE

A parable describes an airplane, superbly equipped for its job, serenely sailing through the blue air, with a hundred passengers on board. One of the passengers, who is sitting at the aisle, is taking out a big black cigar, and puffs the heavy smoke into the plane, almost choking the air conditioning system. The stewardess asks him kindly to stop since this is against regulations, but he pays no attention. She calls the Captain who asks him to stop, with no result. The man looks at him as if saying, "Try to stop me," and puffs on. Everybody is coughing. Then the man in the aisle opposite the smoker takes out a big black cigar and starts smoking too. Everybody coughs even more. The Captain says: "I have to order you both to stop smoking. It is against regulations." Finally the first smoker deigns to answer and says: "This is not a cigar; it is a bomb. When I am halfway, pointing with his finger to the half-way mark, "it will explode." Whereupon the other smoker speaks up and says—addressing himself to the Captain and the passengers: "Don't worry, for mine is also a bomb. When I am half-way it will blow up too—and I'll be there before the other, for I smoke faster." And both go on a smoking race, big black mushroom-like clouds envelop the passengers. At the end the Prologue asks what the passengers do, and ends with the words, "You ought to know. You are one of them."

INTRODUCTION

The introduction shows the horrors of the past for whose abolishment revolutions have been fought throughout the ages: slavery, serfdom, torture, persecution, and finds that the horrors of our age are worse than any of these. All these horrors were perpetrated by sovereign states— Sovereignty being the State's power over life and death. Since the horror of war is still with us, in the monstrous form of thermonuclear war, all the revolutions of the past were, in comparison, against puny horrors and were puny revolutions. To make the true revolution is up to us: The revolution against war.

CHAPTER I

Chapter I begins with my birth on January 27, 1910, in Bendlerstrasse, Berlin. I develop every one of these words, "birth," "January 27," "Bendlerstrasse," "Berlin." First, birth. I have to introduce myself to the reader, for he and I are very intimately connected. There is nothing more intimate than to die and we may have to die together. Usually people die each in his own allotted time which is laid down in the genetic pattern of their cells developed in trillions of years of evolution; but sometimes people have to die together, as in airplane disasters. I describe such a disaster and define disaster as something where many have to die together (as opposed to an accident where one or a few die). Usually people die together when something has gone awry, either in the technological system which man has created, or in the natural system which God has created, of water, earth, and stars. The system in which you, the reader, and I may have to die together is an artificial system, not to be found in nature, a human construction. It is the system of national sovereignties.

On my birthday the streets were decked out with bunting, the flags flew from all the windows, garlands were wrung around the houses, for it was also the Emperor's birthday. It was a beautiful spectacle; and a glorious one, for people took its unreality for reality. They thought the spectacle was not only beautiful, but it represented the truth of their existence. Actually, it was all theater and the system of which it was a part came down to earth, in the mud of the trenches, within 4 1/2 years.

On this great day the birth of a baby meant, in terms of the system, little except a new soldier for the Kaiser. It thus had its intrasystemic value—which was no value at all, as it turned out when the baby was 4 1/2 years old. And yet, this birth and others like it, was one of the few true realities of the day.

I then go on to describe my fellow celebrant, the Kaiser, and the system of alliances and counter alliances of which he was heir; thus preparing the way for the fifth Chapter, where I show that Dulles was the new Bismarck and the system has not changed since the day of my birth. Politics is just as it was then, only more so. Also, I prepare the way for the distinction between reality and unreality; for the categories of value—systemic, extrinsic and intrinsic value—which will be developed in Chapter II; for the nature of genes and chromosomes which will become important in Chapter III; and I give the reader an effortless insight into the play of power politics in such a way that he must say, "My God how crazy were these people," for he sees it all from a distance—only to get the shock in the fifth chapter where it is shown that he himself is part of the very same system multiplied a million times, right at the moment of reading these lines. So much for January 27, the Emperor's birthday and mine.

Now "Bendlerstrasse, Berlin." It so happens that I was born in the complex of houses which later became the German War Ministry. And this gives me an opportunity to show the terror, mud, and grimy horror of the trench warfare of the first World War; and to show the new weapons which came into us, such as tanks. This is already prepared for in Chapter I, where, for example, the Prussians win the Battle of Koeniggraetz because they had a breech loader, whereas the Austrians still had a muzzle loader. I show the arms race leading up to the first World War, and the almost literally identical arguments then and now.

I continue the way into the Atomic Age with my school time in Munich, the German revolution and Hitler. Again, all is told in terms of my own experience, always going backward and forward in history from the focus of this experience. In Hitler at school I saw evil organizing itself and I made it my life's work to organize good. This made it necessary for me to know the nature of good and evil; and hence the subject of Chapter II.

CHAPTER II

Chapter II explains my search for the nature of good and evil, occasioned by my experience with the Nazis and by my thinking about the meaning of Freedom. Freedom, I find, simply means "being able to," the power to act; and it has many degrees. There is formal or intellectual freedom, the freedom to think. There is physical freedom, moving the limbs of the body, in health; and unfreedom in sickness and torture. There is material freedom, of moving the body in space, and unfreedom in prison, in passports—by that time I am already a refugee—and in poverty which I came to know by experience. I understand why Voltaire said: *"J'aime l'argent parceque j'aime la liberté."* And there is freedom of one's own self, of being what one is, and the unfreedom of not being one's own self—spiritual freedom and unfreedom.

I then use the notion of freedom to develop the three dimensions of value, systemic, extrinsic, intrinsic, and to discuss the nature of good and evil. In particular, I show that it is evil to use bad means for so-called good ends; that bad means corrupt the ends; for example, no cause justifies murder. I apply the notions of Freedom and Value to individuals and nations, asking who is free and who is unfree and in which way. It turns out that in different nations people are free and unfree in different ways. In Nazi Germany, the Dominican Republic, Nicaragua, Franco's Spain and Stalin's Russia they were sometimes not even bodily free, but most of them were. In no nation are the majority of people spiritually free, or even conscious of what this means. Thus, I show the degrees of freedom and, connected with them, the three dimensions of value and the nature of good and evil. All these have degrees; and the world is not "half slave and half free." Even in the pre-Civil War U.S. South most people, including slaves, had bodily freedom. And how shall one weigh spiritual unfreedom against physical and material freedom? Jesus did it clearly; and He weighted spiritual unfreedom more heavily than physical or bodily freedom.

By that time, in my development, the Second World War, in which evil personified itself in Hitler and his heeds, has come and gone; and I return to my house in Munich and to the rest of Germany asking myself: "How did this disaster happen? What was the fatal system and how did it come about? What went awry? How could people march so blindly, and fiercely, to their doom?" Thus we come to the third chapter.

CHAPTER III

The system in question, I concluded, was that of sovereign nations. The wrong of sovereignty is that it gives power over life and death. This aspect of Sovereignty I called "Supremacy," keeping the term "Sovereignty" for the administrative authority exercised in a territory. I made all these meditations in, and at the occasion of, the German ruins. A nation is an administrative unit and does not have to have the power over life and death. General Motors or the City of New York do not have it; but the medieval cities had it. To give the power over life and death to any administrative unit is an over-valuation of this unit; it is fetishism and idolatry. How did the state get this power? I went back in history to the very source of it: On October 28, 312 A.D., a Roman Emperor, Constantine, thought that the Christian God of love would make a more powerful God of Battle than any other god. He won, and from that day on, the God of Love became a military symbol, degraded to the level of the state, rather than the state becoming lifted up to the

God of Love. I then follow the course of sovereignty, through the revolutions designed to abolish its evils, finding that from every revolution Sovereignty arose strengthened and renewed like a Phoenix out of the ashes (as is seen strikingly in the new nations today, e.g. Ghana). Every victor in a revolution is eager to grab so powerful a tool for himself. I looked into all the theories of sovereignty and found them all wanting; they all elevate the system of the state over the individual who is the state's subject.

It was, thus, necessary to find a new notion of Sovereignty. The problem was perplexing; how could one preserve the State's administrative authority over a territory and hence its citizens, and yet make the citizen, as a human being, supreme over the State which is merely a construction by human beings? How could one make human liberty by the very mechanics of the state, into the state's supreme value, rather than leaving the state's autocratic conception intact and having human liberty "tolerated" or "guaranteed" by the all-powerful state? What then, I had to ask myself, was the true law of the formation of states? I thought of this problem for many months during my visits in Germany, discarding one theory after another. One day, while walking along the Loenigsallee in Duesseldorf, I happened to notice a policeman at a street corner. And suddenly the solution came to me. This policeman is the representative of the State's sovereignty. What is his function? To help out in emergency. Why do we pay him? Just in case—in the hope that we will never use his services but that he may help our neighbor if and when he is in trouble. We thus, in effect, finance the State's aid to our neighbor. The principle in question is none other than the insurance principle. The state is an insurance corporation for those purposes for which private insurance companies have an exemption clause—namely large-scale disaster, so-called acts of God. The state is a disaster insurance corporation. (Cf. Time, of Nov. 11, 1961 on British Honduras, as an interesting confirmation of this thought). I suddenly understood why in every rubble field of a German city the few gleamingly new buildings were insurance companies. I describe how I developed this new notion of sovereignty, writing to all the insurance experts in the country, and how I elaborated the theory in all its details, including, in particular, the feature of insurance swindle, the invention of an emergency when there is none. This means the swelling of the State apparatus, especially the military bureaucracy, by inventing an emergency and an "enemy." I show how useful is the existence of Russia for these purposes and demonstrate that our image of Russia is largely our invention, as vice versa Russia's image of America. Neither image has much to do with reality. It is no exaggeration to say that we don't have the military establishment because of the Russian threat, but that we have the Russian threat because of the military establishment. The new frontiers, therefore, must be new fronts, not horizontal, like this:

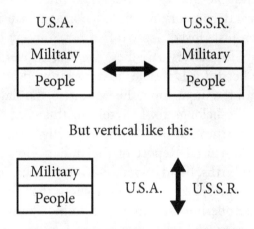

But vertical like this:

The Peoples of the world must unite against their united military. They have nothing to lose but delusions and ultimate disaster. They have a world of peace to win. The new front is actually that between the spirit of life and the sameness of death.

I go into detail into the way the military help each other, the international of Sovereignties. Like communicating tubes, when the liquid rises in one it rises in the other. This leads to Chapter IV.

CHAPTER IV

Here I show the true nature of thermonuclear war. Every chapter has a motto and the motto of this chapter is from Candide: "Well, my dear Pangloss," said Candide, "when you were hanged, dissected, severely beaten, and tugging at the oar in the galley, did you still think that things in this world were all for the best?" "I am still as I always have been of my first opinion," answered Pangloss. I show the horror, making it even more horrible by "humor," ala Kahn. And I make it ridiculous by showing it to be a direct development of the muzzle loader and the breech loader. The thinking of the military and their "experts" is today just as circumscribed and systemic as it was at the time of the old Prussians, only that this time it will be the whole world that will be blown up. Hence the grisly transposition between the triviality of Kahn's thought and the cosmic power he speaks of. The nature of thermonuclear war is of course, controversial; but so was the abolition of any past evil, e.g., torture. I quote the arguments for torture, as a blessing of the soul, from historical documents; for child labor, as a beautiful education which the children just "loved" (so wrote a Dr. Andrew Ure, in 1835); and the arguments for slavery. All these were controversial subjects. I make a nice wide berth for Dr. Teller to move around in, and give him good company with the inquisition, the exploiters, the slave traders, and all the rest which he belongs to. I myself, in this controversy, am for common sense and simple reason. I show exactly—and my source is the incontrovertible neutral Report of the Indian Government—how many cripples, still births, blind, blood and bone cancer, each megaton suspended in the atmosphere produces. I show that there are almost 100,000 megatons (one hundred thousand million tons) of explosives stored at this moment, and what this means for life on Earth. And I point out that ever more bombs are being produced every minute and second, as you are reading these lines. I follow the arguments for the nuclear balance of power showing that they are sometimes literally the same as those the reader found so silly at the time of my birth. I discuss the tragedy of America which has become the New Prussia, and I quote Washington's comment on today's situation, which he foresaw. This leads to Chapter 5.

CHAPTER V

The gist of this chapter consists of three points. First, that governments are, according to all constitutions instituted to guarantee life, liberty, and the pursuit of happiness—which agrees, at least in purpose, with the insurance principle. Nuclear governments today prepare the death, and the imprisonment in shelters and poisoned air, and pursuit of misery, of a ragged, maddened band of nuclear survivors. I show that these survivors will be cast on their own individual resources in a disaster without measure, and that hence government not only breaks down and relinquishes its obligation to protect in emergency, but, on the contrary, is bringing about the emergency. I then show the moral, legal, spiritual, physical, philosophical, religious, metaphysical and military illegitimacy of this kind of non-government. Secondly, I say, there is only one people which has freedom in the full sense of the word as well as horror in the full sense of the word, the American People. They can use their freedom to end their horror. I go into all the arguments for and against giving up the instruments of terror and show that it would be an inspiring example for all nations throughout the world. It would not be unilateral disarmament but a revolution against the system of obsolete sovereignties—arrogated supremacies over life and death. It would be a return to the roots of the American nation (and radical in this past sense) and it would be a breakthrough to the new frontier of spiritual power, exercised by a whole people (and radical in this future sense). It is America's one and only opportunity to lead the world. In material power her days as the leading nation are numbered; partly because of her limited size and resources, partly because Americans are at heart a civilian people. If it loses this opportunity it will surely perish. If it takes it, it will probably survive. If it should perish in the latter case, it would be because of a perversion of the Russian people who, at the moment when we throw our bombs away, would fire their bombs against us. In this most improbable case we would go down; but—and this is the third point—we would go down anyway if the arms race continues, for it can only end in a nuclear war; and it should be no consolation for us that we tear the Russians down with us into the grave—or rather pull them up into the atomic cloud. This kind of consolation is that of Hitler, when he gave the order to destroy Berlin in his last days. It is demonic, utterly evil. Rather, if we follow the course of goodness, we will produce goodness. And in the unlikely case that we should go down, we would do so knowing that life on earth will at least continue in Russia. We would have made a noble sacrifice for mankind which knows only people. And we would not perish in a senseless accident as otherwise we are statistically bound to do—a wrong button pushed, a message misread, a radar blip misinterpreted—in a disaster as senseless and fiery as an airplane crash. But this case is so improbable as actually never to happen.

The question then is not whether to be red or dead but whether to be alive or dead—whether to be or not to be. Only when one is alive does one have the choice of being red or white or black, whatever one wants to be. Actually, those who blame the ones unwilling to fight Russia as wanting to be rather red than dead, themselves throw up the sponge, despairing of being able to beat the Reds in peace; and they run away from the challenge of life—and of Communism in it—into death. They would rather be dead than having a chance to compete with the Reds peacefully. In order to assess the good will of the statesmen, I analyze them in the light of the values developed in Chapter II. I give a big role to Germany, second only to that of the United States. I end by saying we must become politicians of mankind; and I am prepared to play this role to the hilt. The sword of that hilt being that of the spirit, my country being the earth, and my law the law of nature and of the universe. There is more law between heaven and earth than is dreamt of in our physics books. And so we come to Chapter VI.

CHAPTER VI

In this chapter I design the strategy of man's rebellion against national supremacy over life and death. The first requirement is faith in the goodness and rationality of the world. I prove the world to be so by the insurance principle. For if the world were not primarily good and orderly, most planes would crash, most cars collide, most people be sick—and insurance companies broke. That they are flourishing is a proof that evil and contingency are a statistically small element in the orderly universe. Hence faith is rationally justified. We should have the courage to have faith, faith in faith. Once you have this faith—and my story should help you to get it—you will take seriously the gospel. You will find that we give today what is God's—our lives—to the State and what is the State's—money—to the Church (in weekly collects, if that much). I show how we should reverse this, withdraw our lives—and deaths—from the state, and dedicate them to the cause of man. When nations give wars, we should not attend. I show how simply and easily this can be accomplished, comparing the future revolution with the past revolutions, using the strategy of Gandhi, giving everyone a case to fight for and an inspiration to establish new institutions, to make the earth fit for human habitation, in a new creation. This leads to

Chapter VII.

CHAPTER VII

I explain the new institutions that have to be created. The movement we are going to start, the Movement Against National Supremacies over Life and Death, will have several divisions: legislation, atomic energy, emigration, immigration, conscientious objection, taxation, litigation, education, aid and assistance (especially to victims of wars), revolutionary strategy—in short, it will be the NAACP of the peacemakers, that is, the life makers. This movement is described in great detail so that everyone may find his niche in it. The result will be an ordered earth with its new human institutions; a planetary humanity ready to launch itself into the cosmic adventure. This is the subject of the last chapter.

CHAPTER VIII

Here it is shown that the Conquest of Space is possible only for a moral and unified humanity. The glories of this conquest are true glories, for they concern reality; their system is that of the universe, and the beauty of the universe rivals its truth. The old Sovereignties, in comparison, pale to nothing, their glitter is the tinsel of medals, as against the radiance of the stars. There will be disasters here too, but they will be imperfections rather than the consequence of the system (see Aniara, the new Swedish opera!). At last the best is joined to the greatest—the moral law to the starry sky—and the evil prepared by the military is turned to good use. Evil is overcome by good. The conquest of space will become the moral equivalent of war.

EPILOGUE

The Epilogue finishes the prologue, the stewardess and one passenger simply take the cigars out of the mouths of the smokers and throw them overboard. The plane sails on serenely through the blue sky.

Postscript

When, in the years between 1968 and 1973, Hartman urged the people of the world to rise up and stand against the tyranny of national sovereignty, only five nations had nuclear capability. He wrote mainly of the threat to civilization posed by the nuclear build-up of the two nuclear superpowers, the U.S. and the U.S.S.R.

Our existential situation, he said, was urgent then, with just two nuclear superpowers. How much more urgent is it in 2020 when at least eleven nations now have possession of nuclear weapons and the capability to deliver them to their foes? Each year more nations are striving feverishly to develop their own nuclear capabilities. It's high time that we listen to Hartman, heed his warnings, and figure out how to implement his advice before it really is too late.

My ardent hope is that the publication of the current volume will help to bring about the world of peace that Hartman dreamed of and that he worked all of his life to achieve.

Acknowledgments

The publication of this volume was made possible by the hard work and support of many people. As Editor, I wish to thank each of the following for their role in its development and publication:

The Board of Directors of the Hartman Institute for encouraging and overseeing this initiative.

The family of Bill and Vieve Gore, whose funding of the Gore Summer Research Grants that were awarded to two students and a faculty member of Westminster College during the summer of 2018 made possible the archival research needed to begin this book.

Jennifer Rowley and Polina Lyubavina, two undergraduate students of Westminster College who, in the summer of 2018 dedicated two weeks to conducting archival research that uncovered the essays that comprise this manuscript.

Lacey Kisko, of LaceyAnn Kisko Designs, for designing the interior layout of this book.

Catherine Blakemore, of Treadaway Co. for the cover design and her consultations regarding editing, layout, content, and design.

Vera Mefford, long-time member of the Hartman Institute, for her careful proofreading of the manuscript prior to publication.

Tim McConnehey, of Izzard Ink Publishing, for his guidance and knowledge about all matters related to book publishing.

Arthur R. Ellis and Charlotte B. Ellis for their generous financial contribution which has made the publication of these monographs possible.

With gratitude,

CLIFFORD G. HURST
Editor

Other Works

For more from this author, you can purchase many of the following titles by visiting hartmaninstitute.org/bookstore.

Five Lectures on Formal Axiology (2019)
    by Robert S. Hartman
    Edited by Clifford G. Hurst

Freedom to Live: The Robert Hartman Story (2013)
    by Robert S. Hartman
    Edited by Arthur R. Ellis

The Structure of Value (2011)
    by Robert S. Hartman
    Contributions by Paul Weiss

The Knowledge of Good: A Critique of Axiological Reason (2002)
    by Robert S. Hartman
    Edited by Arthur R. Ellis and Rem B. Edwards

La Estructura del Valor: Fundamentos de la Axiologia Cientifica (1959)
    by Robert S. Hartman

Die Partnerschaft von Kapital und Arbeit: Theorie und Praxis eines neuen Mirtschaftssystems (1958)
    by Robert S. Hartman

CPSIA information can be obtained
at www.ICGtesting.com
Printed in the USA
BVHW071820230321
603272BV00006B/621

9 781642 280395